DATE DUE

GAYLORD M-2   PRINTED IN U.S.A.

CONTEMPORARY FRENCH POETRY

CONTEMPORARY FRENCH POETRY

BY

JOSEPH CHIARI

Essay Index Reprint Series

BOOKS FOR LIBRARIES PRESS, INC.
Freeport, New York

First Published 1952
Reprinted 1968

LIBRARY OF CONGRESS CATALOG CARD NUMBER:
68-20289

FOREWORD

by

T. S. ELIOT

A CRITICAL introduction to contemporary poetry may
take one of two forms, according to the degree of
knowledge of the material that may be attributed to the
audience addressed. If the poets to be discussed are almost
unknown, the critic's chief service is to bring their work
to the notice of readers who are likely to appreciate them ;
and his critical acumen will be most appropriately exhibited
by copious and well-chosen quotation. His main task is to
persuade his readers that his poets deserve their attention,
and to send them eagerly to the poetry itself. If, however,
the authors are already known, his aim may be to help
readers who have some acquaintance with their work to
read more intelligently and analytically, to modify their
earlier opinions, and to perceive more accurately the virtues
and defects of writers already accepted as important.

The area which Mr. Chiari has chosen to cover obliges him
to employ both of these methods. Two of his poets,
Valéry and Claudel, authors of an older generation, are
already famous in this country as they are in France :
there exist a number of translations of both the verse and the
prose of Valéry, and at least two of Claudel's plays have been
presented to London audiences. Two of his poets belong
to a middle generation—Supervielle and Perse—but their
work is not yet so widely known in this country as it should
be. The work of a still younger generation—that of such
men as Eluard, Emmanuel, and Michaux—is known only
to those readers of poetry in England who endeavour to

acquaint themselves with new French verse while the poets' reputations are still in the making at home.

I am tempted to draw a comparison here between the task which Mr. Chiari has set himself, and that undertaken half a century ago by Arthur Symons in *The Symbolist Movement in French Literature*. Symons did perform the function of bringing important poets to the attention of English readers ; and for that reason his book will remain a landmark. As criticism I cannot say that Symons's book stands the test of time. He omitted one or two poets of the first importance—notably Tristan Corbière ; he included one or two writers—Maeterlinck and Villiers de l'Isle Adam—whose reputation is now somewhat diminished ; and even when he admired the right authors, one cannot say that it was always for the right reason. My reason for mentioning Symons's book, however, is to point a difference between the poetry of the epoch which he treated, and that considered by Mr. Chiari : a difference which renders the task of the latter much the more difficult.

With all the abundance and variety of the French poetry of the period to which we attach the phrase " the Symbolist movement "—and the difference of aim, technique and idiom between such poets as Corbière, Laforgue, Mallarmé, and Rimbaud is amazing—there is a certain unity which makes it manageable as a whole. It is not so easy to say in what the unity consists : for the more closely we examine the meaning of the term "Symbolism" the more it comes to seem merely a convenient label, and not a defining term. In part, the unity is due to a common derivation from Baudelaire : but the poets whom I have named were anything but epigoni, and what is interesting is not so much what they got from Baudelaire, but what they made of it. The unity is, in any case, felt ; and the contrast makes us more aware of our own period—that which Mr. Chiari has under review—as one in which common directions have been lacking.

Whereas, therefore, Arthur Symons could treat certain

poets as forming, between them, the outline of a period, so that he had no need to refer to a number of admirable poets much of whose work has permanent value (I mention in passing only the names of Verhaeren, Jammes, Samain, Tailhade, Kahn, Regnier, Viélé-Griffin), Mr. Chiari cannot assign to any of his poets the same representative function. He has, I think rightly, made no attempt to discuss all the poets of the last forty years ; he has omitted some of great distinction. His selection has had to be of those poets whose work he finds most sympathetic ; and, as a personal choice, it omits a number of names one or another of which the informed reader will miss. But to have been otherwise, his book would have had to be conceived on a much larger scale ; it might have become only one of those comprehensive scholarly chronicles which seem to exist only to preserve dull writers from complete oblivion. Had he attempted to perform this task, I do not think that I should have been much interested in the result. I therefore cannot repine at the absence of, for instance, Henri Franck, whose poems deserve a greater fame than they have ever enjoyed. In the same way I only mention the absence of Guillaume Apollinaire (in some ways the most representative poet of one type) ; and the absence of several significant figures of the twenties—Cocteau, André Salmon, and Max Jacob. I could wish that more space could have been given to St. John Perse, not only for the intrinsic value of his poems, but because I think he will prove to have had a greater influence upon Anglo-American verse than is yet recognized. And there are, as Mr. Chiari admits in his preface, other younger poets besides Eluard and Michaux who deserve a place. But I mention such omissions only in support of my contention that the nature of the period with which Mr. Chiari is concerned is such as to compel, in any treatment of this kind, a selection which may appear somewhat arbitrary.

For the period itself is one which, until it can be reviewed in a much longer perspective, must be left unexplained : it cannot be exposed to the reader in a neat and intelligible

order. Even if we consider only the two eldest and most
famous of the poets whose work Mr. Chiari examines, it is
difficult to think of Paul Valéry and Paul Claudel as con-
temporaries. Their technique, their aims, their view of life
are in striking contrast. Even their comparative chronology
is paradoxical. In 1910, when I had my first introduction
to literary Paris, Claudel was already a great poet in the eyes
of a younger generation—my own generation. He had
published *Connaissance de l'Est*, *Art poétique*, and those plays
which appeared in one volume under the general title of
L'Arbre : and I am not sure that these three books do not
constitute his strongest claim to immortality. Paul Valéry,
if known at all, was known only as a minor, late Symbolist
poet whose work was represented in the standard anthology
of Symbolist verse, *Poètes d'Aujourd'hui* of Van Bever and
Léautaud. It was only in 1917, after the publication of
La Jeune Parque, that his name was suddenly illuminated
with glory ; yet curiously enough, while Claudel still remained known only to few readers in England, the fame of
Valéry spread as quickly as that of Proust. Finally, when
Valéry died, in 1945, his death seemed to mark the end of an
age, with greater definitiveness and solemnity than that of
any other European author of his generation could have
done. What Valéry represented, in his total *œuvre*—for his
poetry and his critical and speculative prose form one inseparable whole—was the perfection, the culmination of a
type of civilized mind which becomes, to the post-war
world, increasingly alien. While the work of Claudel
remains, for better or worse, closer to the state of mind of the
beginning of the second half of the twentieth century.

When we turn to the representatives of the middle generation, we find equally little relation between the two poets
whom Mr. Chiari has chosen, Jules Supervielle and St. John
Perse. And neither of them can be associated with either
of their great predecessors. I am very glad that Mr. Chiari
chose these two poets, for there are no two poets of their
generation in France of whose permanence I feel more

assured. But what generalizations can we make, from the work of Valéry, Claudel, Supervielle, and Perse, together with the younger writers such as Emmanuel and Michaux and half a dozen others who were worthy of inclusion, about the place and function of poetry today ? It would be impossible to erect an *art poétique* of the achievements of French poetry in the twentieth century. Perhaps it is as imprudent to attempt to define the condition of poetry today in any one language as it would be to generalize about the condition of poetry everywhere. But at least, when we confine our attention to the poetry of one language, we can speak of it in the more manageable terms of the technical problem. Confining ourselves to these terms, we can I think speak of the present situation of French poetry as corresponding to a *crisis of prosody*. It is a period in which each poet is engaged in his own private experiments and explorations in the endeavour to find the right vehicle, the right vocabulary, and the right versification. Eventually, out of these struggles —and only the poet himself knows how arduous, agonizing, and solitary such effort must be in our time—a common style may emerge in the poetry of a generation to come. Meanwhile, the struggle itself is of the greatest significance for all those readers, in other countries and of other languages, who know that without poetry civilization cannot flourish.

T. S. ELIOT.

CONTENTS

PREFACE

THIS book does not claim to be a complete and exhaustive study of the poetry of contemporary France. It is a tentative interpretation of the poetry of some of the most remarkable modern French poets. If I have left out poets like Jules Romains, Charles Vildrac, Soupault, Jean-Paul Fargue, Jarry, Jean Paulhan, Frénaud, St. Pol Roux, Cesaire, Jean Tardieu, R. Dénos, Prévert, René Char, and others, it is because I have mainly set about to describe some landmarks and not to survey the whole of French contemporary poetry. If I have chosen some rather than others, Eluard rather than Aragon, Emmanuel rather than P. J. Jouve, it is because the latter are not only better known in this country, but also because they are nearer the source of the main current which they follow and they have thus already practically reached their full stature. On the other hand, the former are not only still developing but they are doing so at such a pace that they look as if they may be far more important than the latter. Eluard will certainly be a more important poet than Aragon and may possibly be the most outstanding lyrical poet in contemporary French poetry. As for Emmanuel, he seems to me to be the most promising of the younger French poets and he might write what French literature still lacks, a great epic.

This study is the work of a man who has modestly endeavoured to explain why he thinks that certain poems are more beautiful and more accomplished than others, or why he thinks that some are not good at all. It is easier to say why a poem is good than why a poem is bad, for a good poem is something positive, something which succeeds in giving what the reader expects—æsthetic pleasure ; a bad poem is a failure, a failure to produce the expected magic, a failure which, whatever its causes, can only generate feelings of disappointment and irritation, which are not conducive to analytical research. In the extreme case, when the poem is not only bad, but when the poetic experience has not taken place, the critic has no ground for analysis. He cannot be expected to appraise positively or negatively something which, strictly speaking, has not existed.

I submit my views with humility and with the conviction that any critical appreciation of a work of art can only be, in the end, a personal statement of one's likes and dislikes. This approach can only claim to be objective in so far as it recognizes that there is no absolute objectivity except the residue which one finds in the words, when one has reduced them to their essential core. For although words have meanings and connotations which vary according to the person who uses them, language, which is the living spirit of a people, binds them together by the common emotions which it elicits, and by the traditions which it keeps alive. It is also the instrument by which freedom of thought, imaginative constructions, and critical judgments find expression.

The poems from which I have quoted in the text are set out in the *Selected List of Works* at the end of the book. I wish to thank all the authors and publishers who have allowed me to include these quotations. I am greatly indebted to Mr. T. S. Eliot for his unfailing kindness and encouragement and to Mr. Robert Speight for his interest and valuable advice. I take this opportunity to express my gratitude to the Manchester University Press for doing me the honour of undertaking publication, and to its Secretary, Mr. T. L. Jones, for his helpfulness in preparing the book for the press.

INTRODUCTION

LITERATURE can neither be divided into movements nor mapped out as a vast panorama in which various pieces of landscape fit exactly into one another. Literature is the continuous ; it is a living organism ever growing and developing, and it is also the new, the unexpected. But if one cannot talk of affiliations and relations of causes to effects, it is well worth trying to discover the moments and the poets of the past that have certain affinities with our own time and with what is meant by contemporary poetry.

There are certain aspects of philosophical thought, such as existentialism, the feeling of the absurd, the Bergsonian idea of Time, which underlie much of the poetry of our time, but above all, there is one common denominator which seems to appertain to most poetry of our time, and it is Symbolism. I mean by Symbolism indirect poetry, a poetry which by means of myths and symbols seems to convey rather than to describe the extremely complex emotional and intellectual state whence an experience similar to that of the poet will arise. Such a poetry is, when successful, a poetry of synthesis, a poetry in which the words penetrating beyond the real have an aura of transcendence and rise to the metaphysical plane. Like metaphysical poetry proper, it implies the existence of a supernatural world reflected in the world of the Senses. In good metaphysical poetry the two worlds are more than closely united ; they are fused into the oneness of the poem which reveals in a timeless synthesis a moment of eternity. Metaphysical poetry can, of course, be direct ; a great deal of Dante's, of Goethe's, Shakespeare's, or Racine's poetry is direct ; in other words, it is a poetry of statement,

but a statement loaded with so great a weight of emotion
and thought that it reaches down to the very source of being,
beyond the contingent into the absolute.

> Per piu fiate gli occhi ci sospinse
> quella lettura, e scólorocci il viso ;
> ma solo un punto fu quel che ci vinse.

> Quando leggemmo il disiato riso
> esser baciato da cotanto amante,
> questi, che mai da me non fia diviso,

> la bocca mi bacio tutto tremante :

Here we have indeed simple language without metaphors or
similes, but each word " images " powerfully, and the final
picture of the fate-stricken, forlorn lovers conveys a wellnigh
unbearable poignancy : we are beyond death, at the very
source of what makes Life and Death. Such poetry as this
is very often direct, but it is at the same time a poetry of
synthesis. The poetry of the ballads—English, Scots, or
French—is lyrical, direct narrative, yet moving as it does
on one plane, it is not what we could describe as a poetry
of synthesis or metaphysical poetry. But in the poetry of
Villon, shorn of any unnecessary words, at times marked with
stark realism, yet always bearing the imprint of a supreme
purity of expression, the world of man is one, undivided
in Time and the Eternal. Villon's piercing vision reaches
beyond the world of the Senses towards the supreme force
which can redeem man's failings or condemn him to live
the eternal agony of absolute knowledge and separation
from his maker. The love of the senses torments him, but
he is like Donne, he always sees beyond the flesh the skeleton,
and the harrowing vision of old age, decrepitude, death, and
decay of the body constantly mars his most ineffable moments.
Death, for him, is no dream of the Elysian fields of Ronsard
and the Pléïade, yet he lives and loves, falls and prays, hopes

and despairs, as a man and as a great poet who sees beyond the light of today the shades of tomorrow.

In the sixteenth century there are two main trends, that of the School of Lyons which, although it adopted certain new forms of poetic expression, maintained the " oneness " in sensibility of Villon, and that of Ronsard and the Pléïade. The former is symbolical, the latter more naturalistic, and loaded with mythological allusions and allegories. The slow passage from myth to allegory then comes to an end. The allegory tended more and more towards abstractions and concepts, something which entailed a loss of poetry ; the symbol, on the contrary, retained its richness and its power to call forth the myth. Maurice Scève, who belongs to the School of Lyons, can be described as the first Symbolist poet in French literature. For him indeed the real world reflected the ideal world ; his neo-Platonism anticipates that of Mallarmé, as does at times the concentration of his expression which often has a Mallarméan beauty. Like Eluard he finds in love the only protection against Death and nothingness ; indeed in the works of both poets, in Scève's " Délie " as in Eluard's love poetry, woman is raised on to a kind of superhuman pedestal ; she becomes the life-giver, holding Time in her hands, and she is conceived by both poets not as a creation of the imagination, but as a being of flesh and blood who can make Eternity. Scève's belief in the theories of the Kabbala and in the word as a sign capable of revealing the hidden world, anticipates Rimbaud, while his love of mathematics as Kabbalistic signs links him up with Valéry. He is the first French poet whose poetry shows the contrapuntal device of conveying by the harmonies and rhythms of the verse a meaning different from that conveyed by the words as rational means of communication. We find in it the first attempts to create a state of pure receptivity, whence a poetic experience similar to that of the writer should rise. That was Symbolism before Mallarmé ; Mallarmé went further and ended in giving more importance to the silence between the words than to the words themselves, and in equating silence with poetry ;

silence was, of course, willed like the mystic void of Descartes or of Valéry. Mallarmé's experiments found an echo in modern music and they are not unconnected with the various attempts made by writers ranging from James Joyce to Gertrude Stein and Michaux, attempts which aimed at destroying the logical meaning of the word ; at the same time they bear witness to the fact that the poem must not be received but made by each reader, and that true knowledge is a creative act. From Spenser to Blake and Shelley, the idea of the supremacy of the world of the imagination over what we call the real world has never been absent from English poetry ; on the contrary, in France, after the School of Lyons, it is only with the Symbolists—Baudelaire, Rimbaud, Mallarmé, and others—that the poet could say with Shelley :

> Life, like a dome of many-coloured glass,
> Stains the white radiance of eternity.

Metaphysical poetry analyses and reconstructs into a new unity. It is, above all, a sensuous apprehension of thought or a recreation of thought into feelings. The poet feels his thoughts which become experiences modifying his sensibility. The difficulty of metaphysical poetry arises not from the language, which is simple, but from the structure of the poetic phrase, which has become complex, in order to follow the complexity of the thought, which is not simple and generally entails a synthesis of contraries and opposites.

From the seventeenth century onward, we witness both in England and in France a dissociation in sensibility, which will not be healed until the end of the nineteenth century. In this country Milton, with his magnificent language remote from prose, his choice of themes generally beyond the human, helped to precipitate it. In France the process began earlier, with Malherbe and his restrictive rules, and with the poets of the Pleiade and their desire to consider as poetic, only certain subjects ; by so doing they introduced a division in sensibility which only the great genius of

Racine could bridge.[1] He is the crowning figure of what is possibly the greatest period of Western civilization. Either in a positive or in a negative way, Racine is thus the most important influence in French poetry, and in modern times, from Valéry to Mauriac, numerous poets, novelists, and dramatists still follow his inspiration in poetic diction and in their analyses of the human heart. Poetry is for Racine what true poetry should be, a revelation and a means of imparting a kind of knowledge which shows the weight of

[1] In England the union between religion and nature, the temporal and the eternal, feelings and intellect, prevails through metaphysical poetry up to Milton. The Renaissance and the Reformation which ended the hegemony of Catholic orthodoxy did not abolish the Catholic belief in the continuous interdependence of the eternal and the temporal. Man and nature remained the creations of a God or a Force ever present, ever ready to intervene. With Milton we witness the emergence in literature of a kind of Cartesian separation between God and His creation. God is infinite and unknowable ; only His Son—God expressed, yet finite and infinite—can be known to man. Creation is God's substance, but a substance which, freed from God, must, like Descartes' creation, use its own free will. In France the Renaissance had tended to shift the emphasis from God to nature which became both immanent and transcendent ; in countries where the Reformation was successful, the stress is, on the contrary, on the transcendence of God who becomes separated from His doomed creatures, and whose one hope lies in the Redemption and in God's sustained will to save them. Needless to say, Descartes' division between Creator and Creation, mind and matter, accentuated these divisions which are still felt in our time. The eighteenth century, " The Age of Reason ", is also the age of sentimentalism. Reason is the highest faculty of man, but of an incomplete man. Sentiments can be indulged in, but if they are not submitted to the test of mind, they result in sentimentalism. In fact, sentimentalism is the counterpart of abstract rationalism and materialism, and the nineteenth century illustrates well enough those aspects of " divided man ".

Now, with Science accepting more and more the principle that matter is energy, and with Philosophy accepting more and more the complete interdependence of spirit and matter, we tend to return to the acceptance of the fundamental principle of Christianity that " the Word became flesh ", a principle which was also the foundation of that ancient Greek philosophy which asserted that the world of the senses reveals the Spiritual world. All things are again one, with a common source.

errors and evil separating the individual self from the great
" One " source of knowledge, and by so doing points to
death as one of the means of liberation and also of return to
the supreme Will ; with his great contemporary Corneille,
language is, on the contrary, a means of salvation of the self
and not a means of linking the individual self with the great
" One ". On the whole, his poetry has no metaphysical
ramifications ; the words are instruments and not an end
in themselves ; they are the termini of complex human
experiences containing passions and thoughts analysed and
lived through the conscious process of the words, but they
have no echo, no prolongations and no profound roots in
the depths of the mystery of life. The words with him are
not, as in Racine, the truth, the absolute knowledge, which
no human being can bear, they are not a means of destruction
of the self on the temporal plane, but a means of salvation
of the self in the temporal, which for the Corneillean hero
seems to become the eternal. In these two different attitudes
towards language seems to me to lie the very difference
between Racine, the real poet, and Corneille, the extraordinary master of the dialectic of passions against thoughts,
or of passions against passions, but, nevertheless, always
intellectualized passions. That mastery over words is certainly part of great poetry, but is not the foundation of it.
Revelatory poetry alone can bring about that confrontation
of the individual self aware of its isolation, with the im-
mutable will, which can only resolve itself into death. It is
that aspect of Racine's poetry which links him up with Dante.
In Corneille the words lack that metaphysical background
which can bring poetry to the heights beyond the human, in
Racine the words are all, and beyond them there is nothing
except death and rebirth. The characters reveal themselves
and their actions through words which are implacable : words
which represent the knowledge of what has been and cannot
therefore operate any salvation on the human plane, for, as
knowledge is the past, they always come too late ; they can
only reveal and kill.

Racine seems to have burnt out all the resources of the French language as a poetic medium, and after him poetry could not any longer represent the " whole man ". We had to wait for the Symbolists, Baudelaire, Mallarmé, and others to make the synthesis and to restore oneness to poetry.[1] For the Romantics, the death-wish is in contrast with the life-force ; it is always present, and life for them is the constant contrast

---

[1] For various reasons, from the time of Malherbe onwards, the French language has been deprived of a great deal of its primitive poetic power, and has been more and more purified, one might perhaps say intellectualized. Reduced to essentials, it does not permit those easy passages from prose to poetry, such as are to be found in Shakespeare for instance. Another reason is the French tendency towards the general ; the themes of French poetry are never specifically French ; they are as old as our Western civilization, and have been thoroughly explored and moulded by the consciousness of centuries ; they are themes which have been as much as possible deprived of their " unpoetical " elements.

The result of these differentiations in themes and expression is a division in sensibility and a certain prevalence of rhetoric over imagination. The language of Elizabethan drama, although it is enriched with a profusion of literary allusions, is still the language which encompasses all classes of society. Shakespearian themes are, on the whole, themes which belong to the history of England or of the Christian Western world. The secondary characters are not the stereotyped confidants of classical tragedy, but soldiers and servants who express themselves in the racy imaginative language of urban or rural England (simple people tend to speak in images, while intellectual people have lost the power of imagining). It was Milton's language and choice of themes which brought about a division of sensibility in English poetry which was to last until Wordsworth's Lyrical Ballads. Dryden thought that the refined poetic medium of the Augustan age could have improved Shakespearian tragedy. He failed to see that violence expressing itself in a magnificent, and what one might describe as " groupconscious " language, is not sufficient, and leans heavily towards rhetoric ; yet he was a poet great enough to be able to fuse poetic force into words which lacked emotional depth and metaphysical resonance. In the eighteenth century, both in this country and in France, conventionalism in theme and language, together with absolute rationalism on the one hand, and sentimentalism on the other, threatened to swamp poetry. Blake, Wordsworth, and the other great Romantics restored oneness to English poetry.

between what they have and what they would like to have,
or else they would no longer be Romantics, therefore the
death-wish is part of their selves.   Goethe alone solved the
problem by integrating Faust's longings into the transcendental life which contains death and evil.

If we now consider the poetry of our own time we notice
first of all the aspect represented by Valéry who in avoiding
the pitfalls of Mallarmé's extremism realized his master's ideals
and in some ways linked up contemporary French poetry
with the highly intellectual poetry of the sixteenth century.
Then we have the trend represented by the poets of the
Christian myth, Claudel, Emmanuel, de la Tour du Pin,
P.-Jean Jouve, Jean Cayrol, Jean Marcenac, and others.   These
poets have something in common with the Protestant writers
of the sixteenth century, d'Aubigné and du Bartas.   The God
whom they all worship is the God of the Bible and of the
Covenanters, the God who stands by their side, seldom the
God of mercy and forgiveness who died on the hill of
Calvary.   D'Aubigné has most of the time what Claudel has
at times, an apocalyptic voice conjuring up biblical visions.
But d'Aubigné can live or breathe only in storms or in the
thick of the darkest night ; it is only in such situations that
he can rise to the summits of lyricism and while most poets
of his time sing of love and revelries, he lives in a world of
fierce struggles seeking to shelter his defeated God from the
destructiveness of men.   With Claudel, God is triumphant
and he is at one with the poet in the act of creation.   The
main difference between those Protestants and Catholic
writers, lies in the fact that instead of the Protestant separation of God from man, the " I " and " Thou " of Karl Barth,
the French Catholic writers are at one with God, in the act
of poetic creation by the word.   Creation is by essence
divine and the poet with his magic power over the words
created by God, when he creates with poetry the ultimate
reality, reaches eternity.   Amongst those poets Jean Cayrol and
Emmanuel are possibly, owing to their experiences, the only
ones who could say with Blake :

Come God not the God of wrath but the God of mercy

But generally Christ the Redeemer and Forgiver, born as
a challenge to Evil and rising triumphant over it by the
sublime power of His self-sacrifice, is most of the time absent.
In one respect these Catholic writers could be described as
existentialists, Christian existentialists, of course, for, like the
existentialists, they seem to believe that life is a continuous
creation, a continuous surge out of nothingness towards the
future, which, by definition, is inseparable from the past,
and which is thus a continuous present. But these Catholic
poets believe that human actions are not intrinsic manifestations of the sense of responsibility and of the will of man
condemned to be free, they believe, on the contrary, that they
are attempts to transcend everyday life, in order to reach by
poetry the Eternal, which, consciously or subconsciously, they
know to exist, and to direct their lives. That attitude implies
both the transcendence and the immanence of a God whose
divine Grace is always ready to lift up His creature to Him.
The Temporal and the Eternal are again closely linked
together, as they were in the Middle Ages. The Catholic
poets seem to have certain æsthetic affinities with the Surrealists with regard to their method of writing ; their faith
in inspiration from on high resembles the Surrealists' absolute
confidence in the subconscious. But the difference is nevertheless very marked, for, although those Catholic poets show
at times a certain exuberance of language, and although they
recognize the value of the subconscious as a source of inspiration, they all seek, in varying degrees, to submit their inspiration to the unifying control of reason.

Another important trend of contemporary French poetry
is the Surrealist. It groups poets like Eluard, Aragon, Jouve,
Desnos, André Breton, and others. Surrealism has, as far
as we can see, no literary links with the past. Though
Baudelaire in his analysis of Poe's poetry had certainly antici-
pated it, it can be said to have begun with Rimbaud ; it is
really a development of modern conditions and of the beliefs

of modern man. Rimbaud owes little if anything to the
past ; he came to literature in a meteoric fashion and probably
in a kind of dazed state. When he awoke he stopped
writing. Surrealism begins with him. Lautréamont of
course had contributed to it, by seeking to reach, often
through artificial means, the state of non-consciousness in
which Rimbaud seems to have been for a part of his life.
Some of the tenets of the Surrealist doctrines were accepted
before the word Surrealism was ever mentioned. The belief
in the union of the irrational world, or rather the world
beyond reason, and reality is neither less nor more arbitrary
than the belief in the union of the rational world and reality.
Blake believed that the only way of penetrating to the true
reality was not by reason but by imagination, but he did not
discard the principle of selective consciousness as is shown by
the cohesion of his poems and his mastery and control over
his symbols. If obscurity there is at times, it is not due to
uncoordinated verbalism but on the contrary to the extraordinary flights of his imagination and to his attempts to find
symbols and images for visions which until his appearance
had remained beyond the range of mind. Coleridge wrote
" Kubla Khan " as if in a dream or having recovered through
an act of the will the experience of a dream. But there are
no Coleridges or Blakes in French literature, and Surrealism
is a literary creed which is out of the main line of development of French thought and of the French language, and
might be considered as a reaction to them both.

Poetry is language, but language loaded with the maximum
of meaning and musical wealth so as to have the maximum
of conjuring power to bring to life visions of eternity. It
is an attempt to conjure up with words what lies beyond
words, an attempt which thus can only be a partial, but never
a complete success. The Surrealists not only believe that the
source of poetry lies in the subconscious, but also that the
poetic act should be completely freed from any rational
control, and be automatic. And so most of them offer us the
amazing flights of their imaginations, untransmuted by

language.   They fail to realize the importance of that simple
truth which both Blake and Mallarmé knew so well, the
truth that poetic activity does not consist in clothing fantastic
visions and experiences in words but on the contrary in
releasing from the words-symbols the eternal which they
contain.   Poetry is really the liberation of language, and
just as God the Creator is the supreme consciousness, the
poetic act which creates with the word must also be an act
of consciousness.   And it is a fact that poets of merit like
Eluard and Aragon in France and Dylan Thomas in England
soon realized the importance of consciousness and sought to
combine the maximum freedom of inspiration from the
subconscious, with the minimum control of consciousness.
A poem aims at creating by the mechanism of rhythm a kind
of receptive state similar to that of a medium in a trance,
so that the poem itself may be born.   That kind of state
cannot come about unless, once a certain pattern and rhythm
are adopted, they are sustained to the end and thus produce
the necessary relaxation for the birth of the expected mystery.
If there has not been any selection in the process of creation
the words which will have sprung as in a kind of spontaneous
generation will not have that incantatory value ; they will
either be completely hermetic or at best drag the reader
through an exhilarating sequence of images.   This will not
form a poetic experience although it may be, one must admit,
a good mental exercise.   If absolute Surrealism is at all
possible, its only field of partial success seems to be that of
painting, where the exhilaration of colours, whatever their
sequence, or the abundance of the themes, whatever the
pattern, may still offer to the imagination of the silent
observer the possibility of extraordinary and moving experiences.   One cannot fail to note in passing the existence of
a striking relationship between Surrealism in art and Communism in politics, for it is a fact that the best Surrealist poets
like Aragon, Eluard, or great painters like Picasso, are closely
associated with Communism.   The main explanation for
such a relationship might lie in the assertions of André

Breton, the theorist of Surrealism, who believes in the existence of poetic determinism governed by the same laws as Dialectical Materialism and endowed with the same ineluctability. Breton, who sneers at Western thought, declares that everything must be changed, made anew, and that every means must be used to bring about the ruin and the destruction of the ideas of family, motherland, and religion. He thus joins hands with certain rather dubious interpreters of Marx.

Poets defy even the vaguest classification. Writers like Supervielle, St. John Perse, Reverdy, and Michaux cannot even be included in any one of the very fluctuating main trends of modern French poetry. Naturally they have many traits in common with the poets already mentioned but, as I hope to show in the course of this study, above all, they stand on their own.

I

PAUL VALERY

VALERY is one of the major poets of modern times, the most accomplished and, with the exception of Baudelaire, possibly the most important French poet since Racine. Victor Hugo may have soared to greater heights than Valéry or Baudelaire, yet, in spite of his extraordinary imagination and wealth of words, he lacks that supreme consciousness and subtly discriminating taste which could have transmuted his powerful imaginary flights into such complete achievements as " La Jeune Parque ", " Le Cime-tière Marin ", or " Fragments du Narcisse ". " Ce que dit la bouche d'ombre " contains samples of much greater poetry than we can find in Valéry, but " La Jeune Parque " or " Le Cimetière Marin " are more accomplished poems, and as they are on a high level, they could be considered as greater poems. One of the elements of greatness in poetry seems to be that it appeals to all levels of the human intellect and sensibility, and at all times. Such is the poetry of Shakespeare, Dante, and such is on the whole, the poetry of Milton. But a universal and sustained appreciation is far from being the only prerequisite of great poetry. There are poems that give satisfaction to only one kind of reader and yet they are undoubtedly great. Such are some poems of Blake, of Wordsworth, or part of the poetry of Racine, yet who would say that " Phèdre ", " Athalie ", and " Andromaque " are not great poetry ? Valéry's poetry has a Racinian purity, a kind of ethereal elevation which does not appeal to all readers, but " La Jeune Parque " and " Le Cimetière Marin " are as near as possible to great poetry, for there the magic of words contains, in an objectified form, the source of the greatest themes which have always occupied the human consciousness.

It is difficult and probably unwise to come to Valéry without halting for a few brief moments with his master Mallarmé. Consciously or unconsciously, Mallarmé's ideal was Blake ; their poetic beliefs were indeed strangely similar. The neo-Platonism of Mallarmé, his belief in the existence of an eternal world with which the very essence of man is one, is close to the " One Man " of Blake. Both distrust reason and its products—ideas. They believe that the truth lies not within the realm of the comprehensible but, on the contrary, in the imagination and that it must be brought to life with words. The world of the senses, say Mallarmé and Blake, is a distortion of the true world : and Poetry, which is

> To see a world in a grain of sand
> And a heaven in a wild flower
> Hold infinity in the palm of your hand
> And eternity in an hour

is the only way to that eternal world. Blake's or Mallarmé's approach to poetry is a mystical one. It is only by complete surrender, by the abolition of the self as Blake describes it, that we can reach God or " One Man ". Blake wrote poetry without trying to explain how that surrender could be brought about. But Mallarmé, who possessed to an extreme degree the theorizing tendencies of the French, explained at length in his conversations the means by which one should seek absorption in the absolute beyond the consciousness of the self. Poetry, according to Mallarmé, is successful in as far as it is purely music. For music is indeterminate and poetry should be music and nothing else. In order to achieve that aim, to create the eternal which lies beyond our understanding, the poem must seek to avoid concreteness, and the words, deprived of their contingent meaning by all kind of syntactic distortions, tend more and more towards expressing only the very essences of things, and thus come nearer and nearer to the perfection of silence. But since it is impossible to eliminate completely the meaning from the word, poetry is by definition a failure and can only be achieved by accident. Yet in that definition of poetry lies the whole Symbolist doctrine that poets had to try to produce music with words which are not musical notes and unlike them, have a rational meaning. But it must be understood that the music is not in this world but in another world, beyond reach, in silence. The words are prompted by sensations which are really the perceptions of actions which take place in that other world ; so that the words are the symbols of the unknown reality and could, if used properly, that is to say poetically, enable one to reach it. The problem for Mallarmé was to create, with the poem, silence ; an impossible task.

For Valéry, poetry is not music composed to abolish consciousness, but is on the contrary a construction, an architecture realized through an effort of supreme consciousness. The poem itself is that consciousness which is the very essence of the mind, apprehended intuitively in its process of continuous working. Valéry's poems are the record of these continuous assertions of consciousness which are obtained by the exhaustion of every creative effort of the mind in an attempt to reach the transcendental self, and this self is really the mind in its activity.

That pure consciousness, that capacity for burning out ideas, Valéry sought to embody not only in all his works from " La soirée avec Monsieur Teste ", through his poetry, " Fragments du Narcisse ", " La Jeune Parque " right up to " Faust ", but also in his life. Both as a man and as a poet, Valéry sought to remain in a constant state of virtuality and formlessness, fascinated by the unrealized possibilities of his infinite self :

> Mais moi, Narcisse aimé, je ne suis curieux
>   Que de ma seule essence ;
> Tout autre n'a pour moi qu'un cœur mystérieux
>   Tout autre n'est qu'absence.
>   " Fragments du Narcisse."

That refusal to be anything, that detached attitude born of the awareness of the limitations of the intellect, always prevented him from adhering to any political, literary, or metaphysical creed. That identity of man and poet is not difficult to understand if we bear in mind that, for Valéry, art was not only an expression of the artist's personality, but also a means to realize that personality to the full.

For Valéry the problem of creation always involved the process of passing from the chaos of non-being to the ordered form of being. That process of creation is the highest form of consciousness and the only way of revealing the self, or rather of being conscious of one's self; that is to say of one's existence.

Valéry, like Sartre, believes that it is in the continuous process of passing from non-being to being that man's consciousness and liberty resides. But while Sartre sees man as gratuitously condemned to be free, Valéry, finding that all philosophical propositions are purely a matter of language, that all philosophical creeds are at the same time defensible and subject to refutation, refuses to adopt any doctrine or dogma. He chooses to remain at the centre, in a state of permanent disponibility, with his Self as the ceaseless fire which consumes everything, which lights the human road of personality and produces the ashes which are his poetry. Valéry, in contrast with Sartre, places the emphasis not on existence but on the consciousness of existence. He remains a Cartesian who could say "I think or I create, thus I am." Yet if Faust's famous confession to his Secretary Lust—" Je respire et rien de plus car il n'y a rien de plus. Je respire et je vois " (" Mon Faust "—Act 11, scene 5)—can be taken to reflect Valéry's beliefs, Valéry at the end of his life seems to have reached the philosophy of existence. But bearing in mind the fact that Valéry wanted to be " un penseur par excellence "— the light ever ready to shine in any direction, one understands why his thought and his attitude of mind are rather static. Nevertheless, this development is no surprise to anyone who examines Valéry's life and poetry. At the beginning of it we find a refusal to be anything, not even a poet ; and so, after a few poems, we have a silence of twenty years. This is broken at last by " La Jeune Parque ", which is amongst other things one of the most personal experiences in poetry ; and through its five hundred lines, some of them among the best ever written, we have all the aspects of the struggle between being and non-being, consciousness and chaos, mind and matter, ending with the words :

> Alors, malgré moi-même, il le faut, ô Soleil,
> Que j'adore mon cœur où tu te viens connaître,
> Doux et puissant retour du délice de naître,
> Feu vers qui se soulève une vierge de sang
> Sous les espèces d'or d'un sein reconnaissant !

echoed by the end of the " Cimetière Marin ".

> Le vent se lève ! . . . il faut tenter de vivre !

The greatest divergence between Valéry and his master Mallarmé and the symbolists is over the idea of Time. For Mallarmé as for Blake, Eternity lies beyond ; it is the eternal ideal to be recovered, with Blake by the abolition of the self, with Mallarmé by the incantation of the poem. Consciousness and self-consciousness must be abolished to reach silence and eternity or non-being. Blake of course said that " Eternity is in love with the productions of Time ". He also realized that to free the eternal self would mean the destruction of creation. Eternity thus could only exist in Time, for God only exists " in man and living nature ". For Valéry there is no eternity except in supreme consciousness. He rejects immortality :

> Chanterez-vous quand serez vaporeuse ?
> Allez ! Tout fuit ! Ma présence est poreuse,
> La sainte impatience meurt aussi !
> > " Le Cimetière Marin."

He rejects also the philosophy of the Eternal as unreal, and prefers the philosophy of movement, movement which submits man to the gnawings of consciousness ; but that state is preferable to the state of non-being in which there are no worries :

> Pères profonds, têtes inhabitées,
> Qui sous le poids de tant de pelletées,
> Etes la terre et confondez nos pas,
> Le vrai rongeur, le ver irréfutable
> N'est point pour vous qui dormez sous la table,
> Il vit de vie, il ne me quitte pas !
> "Le Cimetière Marin."

For Valéry the supreme state is the state of consciousness based on movement and tending more and more towards absolute knowledge. It is the state which permits the transformation of non-being into being, and it is the sustained efforts of consciousness in man or in the artist which can succeed in abolishing the accidental and in creating a transcendental order which is the only way of vanquishing Time and reaching the Eternal. In that respect, Valéry could be described as existential. Eternity for him can only be grasped through Time in the supreme moment of creation, when the self transcends past and future and becomes the meeting point of all that has been or might be, for it is placed

> Entre le vide et l'événement pur,
> J'attends l'écho de ma grandeur interne,
> Amère, sombre et sonore citerne,
> Sonnant dans l'âme un creux toujours futur !
> "Le Cimetière Marin."

For Valéry Eternity can only be created through existence, in Time. Non-being is nothing ; it has no attributes. Not even God could bear that state of perfect Eternity of nothingness, and it was only by breaking His unity that He could attain the consciousness and the awareness of Time and thus of Eternity. So consciousness became the temple of Time, and the source of Eternity which can only be known in Time.

> Temple du Temps, qu'un seul soupir résume,
> A ce point pur, je monte et m'accoutume,
> Tout entouré de mon regard marin.
> "Le Cimetière Marin."

It is in the "Cimetière Marin" that Valéry explores the opposition between Eternity and consciousness represented by the sea,

> La mer, la mer toujours recommencée !

and the sun or non-being, "Midi le juste",

> Midi là-haut, Midi sans mouvement
> En soi se pense et convient à soi-même . . .
> Tête complète et parfait diadème.

undivided, eternal, beyond consciousness, the world of the Dead, the world where

> Un peuple vague aux racines des arbres
> A pris déjà ton parti lentement.

But :

> Tu n'as que moi pour contenir tes craintes !
> Mes repentirs, mes doutes, mes contraintes
> Sont le défaut de ton grand diamant. . . .
> "Le Cimetière Marin."

or :

> Alors, malgré moi-même, il le faut, ô Soleil
> Que j'adore mon cœur où tu te viens connaître
> "La Jeune Parque."

Eternity can only live through man's consciousness, through acceptance of life and also acceptance of a certain amount of ignorance. One cannot resolve the enigma of creation. If that supreme knowledge were achieved, it would destroy creation itself.

Consciousness is deadly, yet it is the foundation of man's personality. In every man consciousness is the "Young Fate", fascinating in its variety, its mysteriousness, image of the Self constantly trying to discover its essence. But that desire to know, to reach supreme consciousness turns into a desire for self-destruction so as to return to the essence.

On the other hand, the body which seems in constant contact with all the manifestations of the universe, the wind, the sea, the sun, " Le feu vers qui se soulève une vierge de sang " of " La Jeune Parque " or the stimulating call of the sea of " Le Cimetière Marin " seeks to distract the self from its too long self-contemplation which would be destructive, and brings " La Jeune Parque " to the acceptance of birth and the poet to the acceptance of action.   But that destructive power, source of our greatness and misery (since it is the thought of Pascal), is always in us, making death present and gnawing away our existence.

> Le vrai rongeur, le ver irréfutable
> N'est point pour vous qui dormez sous la table,
> Il vit de vie, il ne me quitte pas !

And the verse which follows makes it perfectly clear that the gnawing worm is consciousness, the very self of the poet :

> Amour, peut-être, ou de moi-même haine ?
> Sa dent secrète est de moi si prochaine
> Que tous les noms lui peuvent convenir !
> > " Le Cimetière Marin."

Consciousness, like " la Parque ", is both deadly and beautiful and lives in all of us, and in " La Jeune Parque ", in the " Narcisse ", and in most of his poetry Valéry has expressed in unforgettable lines the supreme struggle between consciousness or thought, and the soul,

> Harmonieuse Moi . . . Mystérieuse Moi

beautiful emanation of life symbolized by the youthful virgin body full of promises of " La Jeune Parque " or of " Narcisse " who says :

> J'aime, j'aime ! . . . Et qui donc peut aimer autre chose
> Que soi-même ?
> Toi seul, ô mon corps, mon cher corps,
> Je t'aime, unique objet qui me défends des morts.

Though in "Fragments du Narcisse", we already have echoes of that blend of sensuality and pure intellect which composes the greatness of Valéry's poetry, "Narcisse" reminds us of the frigid "Hérodiade" or the impotent eroticism of "L'après-midi d'un Faune". Narcisse cannot love anything, anybody but himself and so, "curieux de sa seule essence", he resigns himself to being united to his "corps misérable" and thus of course breaks Narcisse who disappears.

The struggle for the emergence of consciousness from nothingness is the subject matter of most of Valéry's poetry, which is the record of the process of that struggle taking place in the poet's mind. What counts for Valéry is not so much the work finished, as the way in which it is made, its construction, the mastery of the mind over matter or ideas. Like Leonardo da Vinci, his hero, Valéry was interested not so much in completing a work as in exploring the means to obtain certain results ; in short, he was constantly engaged in perfecting his instrument, adding to his knowledge for knowledge's sake, the power to realize anything. To know is the supreme aim of Valéry,

> A ce point pur je monte et m'accoutume,
> Tout entouré de mon regard marin,

to be capable of creating from chaos the only reality which is eternal. And that knowledge must not lead the poet to accept fixed ideas. On the contrary, he must always preserve his potentialities, he must ever define himself anew ; for consciousness is for Valéry the foundation of personality and it becomes the technique by which any transformation must be attempted. The poet, like the scientist who knows his formulæ, can attempt anything. He can even equate Love with a beautiful little temple, like Eupalinos who represents his beloved by a similar geometrical construction. Thus for Valéry the ideal artist and creator is the architect who aims at satisfying the law of numbers, at giving definite concrete shapes to things, and at making them live by themselves and yet as symbols of ideals which the poet or the architect knows. Form, the opposite of nothingness, is the aim of the artist. To give form is the act of creation, whether on the divine or the poetical plane. The alternative title of "Eupalinos" is "L'Architecte". Dance has just the same value as architecture, for it represents passion, but passion controlled down to the smallest detail in order to create out of nothingness the construction which the mind has willed. We have travelled far from Mallarmé's aspirations towards the infinite and perfect silence.

For Valéry, poetry is simply language, for without language neither consciousness nor poetic creation are possible.

Honneur des Hommes, Saint LANGAGE.

"A poet", says Valéry, "is inseparable from the language of his country; more than any other artist he belongs to his country, and a true poet cannot be translated, for form and content are one." French poetry is the flesh and spirit of the French language. The language maintained alive, purified by the efforts and creations of all poets, is the unifying bond and the living link which holds together all the poets who have written in that language. According to Valéry, "each poet is only a member of the immense choir of living and dead people composed of all the French voices, since there has been a France which thinks and speaks; our poetry is France with all its geographical variety and historical accidents, with all the traits and traditions of the French genius embodied in the French language."

One of the main tendencies of the French genius throughout the ages has been the tendency towards clarity, towards consciousness, the desire to know whatever the cost and to keep a lucid mind even in the most harrowing situations. Lucidity in thought means of course lucidity in expression. Phèdre is conscious of her guilt, she knows that everybody on earth, in the empyrean or in the underworld, knows her crime. She knows that she will have no peace in life or in death, yet she faces with supreme lucidity her ineluctable destiny and she unfolds the agony of her heart in lines of crystal purity. Valéry is in our time the last representative of that Racinian purity and power of expression, and one cannot fail to note how his poetry is haunted by memories of the theatre, and how in the end he could not resist the urge to write dramatic poetry. In his greatest poem, " La Jeune Parque ", which is a meditation of the Young Fate or of the poet's self, Valéry makes use of all the devices of the theatre : the dialogue between the Young Fate and the serpent, the monologue of the Young Fate, the description of the place of the action, and the movements and gestures which have a dramatic flavour in the course of a sequence of psychological situations, not unrelated, as Valéry said, to " physiology ".

" La Jeune Parque ", one of the most difficult poems ever written, is probably the best example of Valéry's poetic method. To construct a long poem which is only poetry and nothing else is an impossible task, and yet the poem must be a whole. " If the poet ", says Valéry, " could construct poems in which the musical continuity would never be interrupted, and in which thoughts like music would flow harmoniously into one another, they would be pure poetry." In reality such is not the case, and there is no absolutely pure poetry throughout the whole length of a long poem. So in a long poem like " La Jeune Parque ", Valéry, who was intent on remaining as near as possible to pure poetry, sought to avoid using a story as a binding element, or to allow the poem to drift into a succession of lyrical stages. He thus chose to have many threads running through the poem, threads which have the same value as the themes of a fugue and he succeeded in sustaining throughout the whole that continuous intermingling of the three planes—the intellectual, the sensuous and the musical. It is a kind of musical representation of successive states of consciousness. Valéry himself has made clear what he meant by poetry. " A poem ", he said, in " Album de vers anciens ", " is a duration in the course of which I breathe a law which has been prepared. . . .

Moved by the word, if the metre which permits a kind of anticipation of the future, binds my memory, I feel the full strength of every word for having waited for it." It is a definition of poetry which disposes of some of J. Benda's criticism, for it certainly makes it clear that the poem is not a haphazard birth of the subconscious, but on the contrary an assertion that, in order that the poem might be born, the mind's receptivity and expectation of the coming word has to be prepared by the hypnotic effect of the rhythm. No poem can be born unless each word which comes is as if expected. That process of creation implies a certain control of the mind, not the verbalism of Surrealism where the words, like the explosions of a munition dump, follow automatically on one another.

Valéry is a true heir of the great classical age. He not only has always present in him the critic who sifts and controls but also the antagonist of sentimental Romanticism. "Narcisse", "La Jeune Parque", have more in common with "Psyché" or "Adonis" and the age of Racine than with Rolla, Elvire, and the age of Victor Hugo.

Pure consciousness is only an hypothesis of the mind. As a state, it cannot be reached. Consciousness is consciousness of something and seems to be realized at the point of separation of the self from the object or thought which engages the consciousness. Thus consciousness is a constant projection forward in an attempt to seize itself and to exist. The mystic who merges his consciousness with God exists and realizes thus the transcendency of the contingent world. Paul Valéry was not a mystic, at least in the usually accepted meaning of the word. For him there is no God. He can only realize himself through the same process as "Narcisse", plunged in the self-contemplation of an ever-elusive Self. But that process is fraught with great dangers. It is the danger that if consciousness could succeed in basing its existence on a unique object, it could also deny the existence of that very object and thus destroy itself. Valéry has described his awareness of that awe-inspiring danger in "La

Jeune Parque ", who at certain moments does not know whether she is going to die or to know. In " Le Cimetière Marin " we witness the same attempt of the self to transcend the human condition,

Quand sur l'abîme un soleil se repose

and in " Ebauche d'un Serpent " that danger is expressed even more clearly :

Soleil, soleil ! . . . Faute éclatante !

The pure self could only be non-existence, and to think too much, to try persistently to discover the sources of life, makes life appear absurd and not worth being accepted. One could apply to the spirit the definition that Æsop applied to the tongue ; it is both good and bad ; it can lead to the sin of Satan and to the kind of intoxication in its absolute, un-disputed power, which if prolonged is a danger to life. Valéry realized that, and he ended by saying " Il faut tenter de vivre ". Life must prevail, and life is movement, more real than the arrow of Zeno, or Achilles' tortoise. He realized that through some yet unexplained mystery or fundamental law which elude us, the very moments when consciousness seeks to realize itself in the state of continuous virtuality, the body, which is the point of contact with and the measure of the cosmos, breaks that ideal and dangerous state of pure spiritual life and brings the spirit down to earth. Indeed it is the compromise between the spirit and the body which makes life. And the human being, the meeting point of Time and Eternity, is ever torn between two forces, that of the spirit towards Eternity and of the body towards the senses. The opposition between being and non-being which was solved by creation remains latent in man and forms the very foundation of human life. The conflict is heightened by the fact that the body and the spirit, in spite of the wander-lust of the spirit, cannot be separated in life. The body remains the soul of the spirit whose dangerous love of

solitude must constantly be broken in order to bring it back
to its moorings, to the form necessary to its existence.

> Sois enfin toi-même ! dit l'Aurore,
> O grande âme, il est temps que tu formes un corps.

And that is the conclusion of the long speculations embodied
in Valéry's poetry ; for in the end it is by his actions, the
realizations of his self, that man is.   Here we are very near
Nietzsche's " volonté de puissance " and Sartre's " necessary
choice ".   Refusing to accept the existence of the concept
of man based on Christian dogma or to probe in the sources
of the origins of man, Valéry and modern philosophers like
Sartre maintain that man is always making himself ; he makes
himself constantly by his choices and actions gravitating
round a Self in continuous process of change, whose only
constant trait is movement towards the absolute knowledge
of the Self, a state which can never be reached.   In the face
of that impossibility, anxiety or *angst* comes over the poet
in his solitude more harrowing than that of Pascal, or Kierkegaard, for though he realizes the need for God, his mind
refuses to accept the idea of a God " who can only be what
man is not ".   Yet the heart desperately longs to know the
foundations and the workings of a power which contains
the universe and is responsible for its creation.   Even Valéry
is bound to acknowledge that fundamental desire and the
fact that the idea of death would make life impossible, if
there was not hope—" Hope on the top of the highest
Tower, looking beyond mind and body " (Rhumbs).

For him as for Sartre the human being is constantly becoming what he is not, and is constantly in the process of not
being what he truly is, and man in constant process of
" making himself " becomes for Valéry the source of
everything, " L'homme pense donc je suis, dit l'univers."

With his more than sceptical attitude towards philosophy
and science, the only form of transcendency which Valéry
allows, and in which he believes—as is proved by his life—
is the transcendency of art.   Convinced sceptic that he was, it

took him a long time even to accept that belief ; it took him twenty years of silence, and his hesitations are reflected in his greatest poems. But the fact that he wrote poetry, conscientious and honest artist that he was, certainly proves that he reached the conviction that art was the only justification of man's presence on earth. We might ask ourselves how a man whose main principle in life was " Le refus d'être quoi que ce soit" ended in being a poet who left behind him poems which are, amongst other things, the genuine record of imaginatively lived experiences. We might ask ourselves if Valéry, with his belief in the supremacy of the pure intellect, simply imagined, without literally living them, those poetic states, in which senses and intellect are blended into poems. No, Valéry could adopt the same attitude towards the senses as the Pythoness towards the God who invaded her ; but he knew, being a poet, that poetry required a surrender of the intellect and a return to the very source of life, to a realm where rational knowledge is abolished,

Dans un état proche de la stupeur,

in a kind of mystical state which is not union with God but immersion in " the primitive sensation of living ". That is the state in which consciousness has been replaced, or rather filled, by the very act of living ; here all the senses co-operate to produce that kind of plenitude and happiness which Valéry expressed so well in his famous autobiographical passage of " Mon Faust " : " Je vis, je respire." This state is the poetic state, in which the poet, linked inexplicably with all the things and persons which surround him, grasps their meaning not through an intellectual process but directly, as if by some kind of visionary power and with the help of strange emanations from the objects which surround him. For him, placed in the middle of the real world, that world becomes a kind of dream ; a dream in which Time is abolished, and everything is new ; a dream which has a meaning more real and more profound than the world of

everyday life ; a dream in which the only task of consciousness would seem to be to keep an unobtrusive watch
over that state, pregnant with meaning, in which the poet
finds himself, to prevent it from being invaded by triviality,
and to make possible the recording of whatever experience
has been undergone. Consciousness no longer refuses to be
anything but movement, but becomes the centre or the
moving focus of a universe of sensations, which harmoniously
gravitate around it and reflect back the radiations and the
music which are the poem.

Valéry, like all important poets, from Blake to Baudelaire
or Supervielle, realized that intellect cannot communicate
the direct apprehension of a living experience. On the
contrary, instead of giving life, it generally dissects and kills.
Strange as it may seem, by different ways, without any other
beliefs but the belief of being without belief, Valéry used the
intellect to maintain that state of permanent virtuality which
was every now and then filled by the poetic experience.
And so the most sceptical of poets, the most unmystical of
poets, adopted the same discipline as the mystics themselves
from the Prophets to John the Baptist, the discipline of the
withdrawal in the desert to a perfect solitude in order to
hear the voice of God, which for Valéry was the voice of
poetry. And for him, as for the other mystics, the mystical
experience takes place through love, a kind of love which
enables the soul to penetrate to the very depth of the thing
or object observed, and to produce the song which is the
poem, in unison with it. " If you look upon things with
sympathy and love you will give them life," he says. To
give life is man's essential vocation. Besides that, Valéry's
belief in the transcendence of poetry proves that he was not
so perfect an atheist as he prided himself on being. His
aphorisms and analytical writings were belied by his very
practice of poetry which is, more than anything else, an act
of faith ; faith in a transcendental world, which is the source
of all things.

In spite of Julien Benda's attempts to deny Valéry admission to the world of intellect and philosophy, Valéry remains one of the most clear-minded of French poets. A kind of symbol of intelligence, a " Monsieur Teste " poet, he is also a philosopher ; a philosopher not in the accepted sense of the word, for Valéry's philosophy was not a logically expounded and co-ordinated system but was only to be found in action. His power of intellectual construction could never be brought to a standstill, it could never accept any solution as final, and he was such a genuine and convinced sceptic that he even doubted his own scepticism. Valéry's philosophy is a philosophy of action and could be summed up in one single line : " the power to make or to create with words ", a power endlessly exercised by his restless mind like the sea " toujours recommencée ". Thus language for him is not an end but a means, the means to create the thought, to produce the light ; and it is to the production of light that he devoted his energy. He was so convinced of the unique importance of the act of thinking and of the fundamental fluidity of thought that he felt that his poems were never finished. He even thought it possible to devote his whole life to working on one single poem, producing every now and then the different stages of that poem.

" Creation is the only way of realizing one's personality ", said Valéry. So from " Narcisse " to " La Jeune Parque ", " Le Cimetière Marin " or " Mon Faust ", we find in those poems the changing aspects of Valéry's personality. " Narcisse " is that constant inward look of Valéry, that dangerous desire to stand still in the contemplation of the Self. " La Jeune Parque " is again Valéry lost in his intellectual isolation in an island of the Mediterranean Sea, witnessing, living the conflict between the call of the senses, the freshness of youth, and the fascinating purity of non-being. It is the struggle between youth and ineluctable fate, it is Valéry and it is also " Everyman " facing the mystery of life with the ever-gnawing consciousness, which in case of prolonged supreme lucidity would mean death, and the final triumph of the unavoidable law of birth. " Le Cimetière Marin " presents the picture of the same struggle, and in " Mon Faust ", Valéry adopting the conclusions of " La Jeune Parque " and " Le Cimetière Marin " which is " to live ", has become at last existential ; and he asserts his belief with the words :

> Je vis . . . Je respire . . . rien de plus.

He took four and a half years to write " La Jeune Parque ", he made about a hundred different copies and ended by calling it not a poem but an " exercise ". Here at last is poetry in perfect form, poetry which echoes the purity of line of Racine and the Attic grace and sensuous imagery of Ronsard—poetry which has the magic of music and which can conjure up at the same time the mysteries of the mind and the haunting charms of a youthful golden goddess as she undergoes the pangs of revelation.

> J'ai de mes bras épais environné mes tempes,
> Et longtemps de mon âme attendu les éclairs ?
> Toute ? Mais toute à moi, maîtresse de mes chairs,
> Durcissant d'un frisson leur étrange étendue,
> Et dans mes doux liens, à mon sang suspendue,
> Je me voyais me voir, sinueuse, et dorais
> De regards en regards, mes profondes forêts.

Here in beautiful lines loaded with an extraordinary blend of sense and intellect, and showing a penetrating analytical mind, we have some of the main traits of Valéry's poetry: the " éclairs " or " ideas ", the control of the senses, the love of introspection, the birth of consciousness :

> J'y suivais un serpent qui venait de me mordre.

The serpent is one of Valéry's main symbols ; it is the insidious sinner of the Bible, who in " Ebauche d'un serpent " tempted even God into creation, but it is also the source of knowledge and of suffering and death. His bite, consciousness, creates the same disturbance in the mind and body as the idea of physical love to a pure young woman. We are not far from the indefinable mixture of feelings ranging from a curious inebriation to the feeling of utter nakedness, dejection,

and despair which overwhelmed Adam and Eve once they
had eaten the forbidden fruit. " La Jeune Parque " is the
poem which not only shows all the poetic resources and
foundations of Valéry's poetry but also unfolds all the various
aspects of Valéry's thought in lines of supreme beauty :

> Je n'attendais pas moins de mes riches déserts
> Tout peut naître ici-bas d'une attente infinie.
> Qu'es-tu, près de ma nuit d'éternelle longueur ?

Especially moving is the speech of " La Jeune Parque " to
the serpent-consciousness which threatens to shake her equilibrium, and the purity of her sleep. This wakening threatens
to disturb her pure intellectual state, and in spite of herself
she is aware that she loves the bite which gave her pain,
and in so doing, she loves the source of that other self which
is being born in her. The beautiful passage beginning with
" Harmonieuse moi . . ." recalls the time when La Jeune
Parque was in a state of heavenly ignorance, one with the
universe and enjoying an ineffable maternal happiness. Yet
within that idyllic recollection of a state which is now no
more, we feel present all the possibilities of pain and conscious
joy to be awakened in her through the revelation of the senses :

> L'arc de mon brusque corps s'accuse et me prononce,

And in spite of all that innocence, somehow, as if self-born,
Death, her shadow in the sun, was gliding silently in her
wake, an ever-present proof of her existence, and of her
consciousness of the idea of Death. For the shadow is the
proof of existence, and it is also the projection of her unavoidable death, that death which spoils for her any possibility
of happiness, whether in actuality or in dream.

> Je pense, sur le bord doré de l'univers,
> A ce goût de périr qui prend la Pythonisse, . . .
> L'ennui, le clair ennui de mirer leur nuance, . . .
> L'aube me dévoilait tout le jour ennemi.

And more beautiful lines :

> Souvenir, ô bûcher, dont le vent d'or m'affronte.

Some with a Mallarméan beauty :

> Ou toi . . . de cils tissue et de fluides fûts,
> Tendre lueur d'un soir brisé de bras confus ?

And then there is the tense dramatic debate between life and death, whose prize is " La Jeune Parque " and with her the Universe, for :

> Tout l'univers chancelle et tremble sur ma tige,

a debate in which life and spring stirring everywhere with growing force seem to deprive Death of its prize.

> Les arbres regonflés et recouverts d'écailles
> Chargés de tant de bras et de trop d'horizons,
> Meuvent sur le soleil leurs tonnantes toisons.

Here the amazing alliteration of the end is like the final crescendo of a full orchestra.

Spring and the desire which lurks in " La Jeune Parque " seem to triumph over death, and so life will continue. But somehow there is a supreme revulsion. Knowledge and consciousness according to Valéry cannot be fertile, neither can the joy of the senses and physical life accept the supremacy of the intellect which is so dear to this poet. So " La Jeune Parque " refuses life and the Gods keep the same silence which met Christ's anxious questions in the Garden of the Agony. A tear, a very human tear, starts to her eyes as she walks slowly towards her fate. That tear is her only reply to the anxieties which succeed the birth of consciousness. It is her only birth, perhaps her only silent prayer, expressed in words which neither she nor Valéry could utter.

> Mystérieuse Moi, pourtant, tu vis encore !

echoes the meditation of the beginning and introduces a new meditation in which life has triumphed over the

> Sombre lys ! Ténébreuse allusion des cieux.

How did that happen, how did the flesh win ? The serpent consciousness reappears to close the circle and to describe

how that evolution took place. It took place in sleep, which
is brother to death. "La Jeune Parque" was betrayed by
the flesh, and the sensuous images reappear.

> Il eût connu pourtant le plus tendre des nids !
> Car toute à la faveur de mes membres unis,
> Vierge, je fus dans l'ombre une adorable offrande . . .
> Mais le sommeil s'éprit d'une douceur si grande.

During that sleep, she has been transformed, she has lost her
lucidity and the memory of her resolution. She has become
another one :

> Au milieu de mes bras, je me suis faite une autre . . .

and while she had lost consciousness in sleep, in the splendour
and sonority of a verse which opened other worlds,

> Quelle conque a redit le nom que j'ai perdu ?

her soul drifted into a dreamlike state, from which she awoke
to find that life had won. And so she welcomes the end of
night, the coming of day, and answering the stimulating call
of the sea she offers her radiant body to the gilding sun :

> Alors, malgré moi-même, il le faut, ô Soleil,
> Que j'adore mon cœur où tu te viens connaître,
> Doux et puissant retour du délice de naître,
> Feu vers qui se soulève une vierge de sang
> Sous les espèces d'or d'un sein reconnaissant !

So ends what is, with the Four Quartets, the most important
poem of our time, a poem whose difficulty and complexity
are the very source of its beauty. These are not due to
hazard or to obscurity ; they are on the contrary the result
of one of the most conscious and sustained efforts which
has ever been applied to poetry, by one of the most penetrating minds that has ever lived.

M. Julien Benda is the only critic who describes Valéry,
who was a true apostle of reason and intellect, as irrational ;
he constantly quotes him side by side with André Breton and

D

the Surrealists. So strong is M. Benda's bias against Valéry that he constantly takes sentences out of their context, and above all treats seriously some of Valéry's most obvious *boutades*. To lump together " Le Cimetière Marin " and " La Jeune Parque " with Surrealist poems is quite certainly an outrage on that reason which M. Benda claims to uphold. Is there anything more opposed to Valéry's conception of poetry than the quotation from M. Léon Pierre Quint's article published in " Confluences "—June 1945 ?

This defends the Surrealism which M. Benda claims to be Valéry's creed.

Je crois que les grandes œuvres proposent une tâche impossible, qu'une doctrine n'est efficace que lorsqu'elle assigne à l'homme des buts qu'il ne peut atteindre, qu'en lui ordonnant de regarder par-dessus l'horizon à travers les nébuleuses. . . .

" Confluences "—Juin 1945.

So intent is M. Benda in including Valéry amongst " the barbarians " (he is here in good company with Proust, Gide, Bergson and others), that he gives to Valéry's words the meaning which suits him, and quotes any witness hostile enough to keep Valéry in the dock. Take his article published in the " Revue de Paris ", February 1946, when he quotes Valéry as saying : " Le Lecteur jouit d'une très grande liberté quant aux idées, liberté analogue à celle que l'on reconnaît à l'auditeur de musique, quoique moins étendue."

C'est une erreur contraire à la nature de la poésie, et qui lui serait même mortelle, de prétendre qu'à tout poème correspond un sens véritable, unique, et conforme ou identique à quelque pensée de l'auteur.

" Variété," III.

This is a perfectly sensible view of poetry, for there are not two readers who apprehend a poem in the same way. But M. Benda, thought-reader, insists that the real thought of Valéry, the thought which he is too afraid to state, is that a reader is absolutely free with regard to the ideas conveyed by a poem. M. Benda interprets and arranges as he likes, forgetting that Valéry has stated time and again that words are not musical notes, and though the poem is a key to an experience, a key implies a lock, a pattern ; for the words have a generally accepted meaning which every poet must take into account. And in order to demolish Valéry's allusions to music M. Benda concludes that Beethoven's, Wagner's, and Debussy's music has a definite and ascertainable meaning. It is difficult to go further. For the last forty years, France has had, according to M. Benda, no poet worth mentioning, except perhaps Aragon and Mme de Noailles ; with due respect to Aragon he would probably have added Béranger and Déroulède if they had been alive. " The real state of a true poet is the one which is most opposed to the state of dream," said Valéry. It was Mallarmé who stressed in art the necessity of intellectual effort and Valéry consciously placed his intellect above everything, including poetry, which was the record of his intellectual explorations of consciousness, semi-consciousness or dreams. But of course he was a poet and knew that one cannot write poetry with the intellect only. There is no poet more remote from Surrealism than Valéry. In his poetry there is no room for spontaneous creation, with the very few exceptions, as he himself says so often, of a single line or a rhythmical pattern which was sometimes given to him and which he completed with words. Without taking Valéry's assertions literally, it is clear that his poetry is above all a construction, a mental effort to subdue the rebellious matter, as it has to be subdued in architecture or in the dance. As the mathematician could create with numbers extraordinary constructions, so the dancer could give life to the mysteries of music. Valéry is a systematic sceptic and seems to have only one faith : reason and its foundation, which is language. And even those foundations, as we shall see later, are sometimes shaken. The work of the mind not only offers the only possibility of transcending time but is the way of creating a reality more true and more varied, than the reality observed through the senses. For Mallarmé the world existed to be expressed in words which could form a book to which he alluded, but never wrote, and the word was the only way of abolishing " Le hasard ". For Valéry the word is the beginning and the source of everything, and since the word is for him reason, even the myths lose their aura of mystery and become the symbols of his personality. No human intelligence has been more obsessed with the secrets of its own sources and ways of writing. No man has thought so much and so profoundly on thought ; no man has been more detached from the concrete and more intent on exploring the most remote springs of the intellect. Valéry has lived in spheres where the rarefied air was so difficult to breathe that even Faust forsaken by Mephistopheles was overwhelmed by the " Superman " of solitude and cast down into a fall towards the place where live the fairies which in the world of beings might give him " un frémissement d'Eternité ". Lust, like Faust, is as Valéryan as any of Valéry's creations. She is the crystal, transparent companion of the nihilist doctor ; she shows no signs of Christianity and is as little human as possible. The devil himself realizes, when face to face with Faust, that all his wiles and supreme cunning, which made of him a prince in the chaos where he reigned, can be reduced to nothing by the human intellect. And for a moment we are bewildered, wondering if that supreme power of knowing, admired by Lust and the disciple, and feared by Mephistopheles, is going to end in absolute nihilism. But Faust ends in asserting that " Vivre, voir, toucher, respirer " are possibilities given to the human being in order to offer him the possibility of duration, and even of an intense feeling of existence. The poem ends with the impression that Faust might have wished to stop " Time " " at a moment of supreme beauty ", a moment which could transcend the intellect and its obsession with knowledge.

Valéry is not a philosopher but an explorer of the mind, an explorer who at times gets lost, but who refuses to cover the same ground twice, a man with few illusions and fewer

beliefs. According to him, in the end all things are equal
and none is worthy of passionate attachment. That is why
he was so opposed to Pascal. Indeed, with a mind capable
of always seeing the general and thus the very essence of
things, a grain of sand is as important as, say, Napoléon,
since one could not have existed without the other, and
indivisible Eternity is the essence of both. Besides, there
are no repetitions in life ; everything is different at each
second ; the whole is ever present for the eternal eye, and
it is a continuous gradual discovery for man's limited perceptions. On the one side absolute vision, all embracing, im-
mutable ; on the other, intelligence, seeking to discover with
false metaphors and false analogies, yet valid for the man
who can pierce through them with the extraordinary light
of an uncommon imagination. It is only through imagination that we can rediscover the essence of things and, beyond
the everyday use of words which shape our thoughts and
personalities into conformity, recover the virginal meaning of
the word which created and which can therefore re-create.
Only imagination can save mankind from becoming, in spite
of a certain permeability of words, static in language and
thought, while everything else constantly changes ; only
imagination can lead to the very source of knowledge.
Valéry described poetry in mathematical terms, but as a poet
he knew that poetry was born of the imagination which
alone can connect the poet with the life of the cosmos.
He believed in the value of the mind, but he realized also
the insignificance of human knowledge, and the fact " that
anybody trying to probe the depth of things was bound to
be obscure, for light ceases a few feet from the surface ".

After the exuberance of Romanticism and the various
reactions against it, such as " realism ", " art for art's sake "
and " Symbolism ", came the optimism of the pseudo-
scientists who believed that, owing to the discoveries of
science, the Golden Age was just round the corner. Instead,
mankind has been brought twice to the verge of complete
annihilation and still shudders at the memory of its suicidal

behaviour. The result has been to a certain extent the emergence of Surrealism and a despair which leads to nihilism. The most representative examples of this movement are Kafka, Sartre, though he may deny it, and, the most clear sighted, the most conscious and the most courageous of them all, Valéry. To Valéry, the world of the senses and the world of the mind were, in the end, vain ; art itself was vain, everything was vain, there was nothing left but the mind watching itself at work on the verge of a most terrifying vacuum in which absolutely nothing could live, not even Mephistopheles. With him, nihilism has nearly become a mystical experience, something which seems unthinkable.

Indeed, this mysticism of the void links up Valéry with Hindu philosophy and Yoga. Instead of the mystical experience based on love and union with God, we have here a mystical experience based on negation and silence obtained after a series of willed intellectual operations. Man can reach by mental processes the state of pure nothingness and may have by that operation a knowledge of the very essence of being surging from that vacuum. Instead of " cogito ", Descartes could also have said " dubito ", and laid the foundation of the liberty to doubt, which characterizes Valéry. It seems to me that this is perhaps one of the reasons of Valéry's affinity with Descartes—in both cases the soul knows itself by an act and this act is the abolition of all acts. Valéry's aim is to watch himself in the pure act of thinking, but of thinking nothingness, and therefore he knows himself by an act which abolishes all acts. The aim of the intellectual process underlined here is to make the void from which the awareness of the existence of the self is negatively transferred into the status of an act which is indefinable and invisible and yet which is the very mind itself at that moment of mystical union with the void. . Here we have an experience of existence attained by not-knowing, the experience which led Valéry to self-knowledge. Descartes went further and accepted God. But it is too easily forgotten that Descartes, the supreme advocate of reason, was essentially a visionary, who discovered in moments of intuitive illumination the true path to knowledge, "the method" of conducting reason in its search for truth. Valéry and Descartes, two outstanding examples of supreme consciousness, were both in their ways mystics. Descartes believed in the validity of his vision and in a God transcendent but not immanent; Valéry believed in the poetic experience, which was for him the intuitive moment revealing eternity. To Valéry the essence of being was knowledge, and absolute knowledge could only be revealed in those flashes of intuition which required the relentless efforts of consciousness to bring them forth at some very rare moments in a man's life. Descartes also had been searching for absolute knowledge, which was for him the foundation of being. The problem which Descartes tried to solve was posited in terms slightly different from those of Valéry, but the methods of approach were strangely similar; the results obtained were closely alike and yet in agreement with their markedly different respective beliefs. Descartes' metaphysics may well have fathered Valéry's scepticism, for it was above all Descartes' rationalism which insisted on the segregation of mind from matter and stressed the separation of the creation from its Creator who, being therefore useless, fell into oblivion. Thereafter reason alone remained, as lonely as a palm tree in a desert, and yet the only point where men could gather and shelter from the torrid light of the sun—a very precarious and desolate shelter without the faith which feeds life and tempers the devouring rays.

One must note that the foundation of the experience of being on "nothingness" makes of Valéry a man of his age —the age of Heidegger and Sartre. The denial of the primacy of being, the substitution of thought for being, as we find it in Heidegger, who bases his metaphysics upon the experience of "nothingness", causes the nausea of Sartre, the absurd of Kierkegaard and Camus, and the complete chaos of Nietzsche. Yet this is, in fact, a secondary and not a primary experience, for not only must there be being and non-being before there may be "nothingness", but there must be being in order to experience nothingness. And we must say that nothingness experienced by the being in time is only in the thought. Valéry probably realized that truth and at the end of his life he asserted, in the words of Faust, the primacy of being in relation to thought.

Valéry was completely detached from everyday problems. He remarked that men do not love one another, and his feelings about love and emotions are expressed in countless aphorisms scattered throughout his prose writings. For him the life of the senses and the emotions could only detract from the pure life of the intellect. "La Jeune Parque", moved by the call of spring and the desire to satisfy her feminine longings, refers with horror to the thought of giving life and of accepting the sensuous life. "Narcisse" had the same horror of loving another than himself. "Monsieur Teste" has the same attitude and is nearly a pure intellectual machine. Yet Valéry accepted social and family life and was from all accounts a most delightful friend. He probably realized that it was impossible to shut out completely the emotional and physical aspects of life and to lead a purely intellectual existence ; that would have meant, in the end, the death of the conscious self which was the very foundation of his intellectual speculations. "La Jeune Parque" remembers all along her long meditation and internal debate, the unforgettable thrill caused by the awakening of consciousness and physical life, and in the end, like the poet in "Le Cimetière Marin", she welcomes the warmth of the sun and the exhilaration of the sea air.

It is also the conclusion of "Mon Faust" which contains Valéry's thought and in spite of his abhorrence of personal feelings is the most moving of his creations. Here Valéry realized the untenable position into which his intellectual honesty and faith in analysis had forced him. Logically, he should have remained what in his "M. Teste" he had failed to be ; a being of possibilities, a capability of being anything and thus a kind of Faust knowing everything ; a man for whom the world is finite, because he knows everything about existence, except the mere fact of existing physically. It is then only that he realizes that his spiritual power requires to be verified by the act of living, and so he ends by considering living to be the criterion of his art.

Serai-je au comble de mon art? Je vis. Et je ne fais que vivre. Voilà une œuvre . . . Enfin ce que je fais a fini par construire ce que je suis. . . . Me voici le présent même.

The man of infinite possibility has become at last only the man of the present. Valéry has travelled along a road similar to that of Goethe's Faust. The thirst for knowledge does not lead him like the first Faust, to death and damnation but simply to death ; and just as the second Faust realized that he could only be saved by action, Valéry realized that man's essence is to exist and to contribute to humanity. Existence can only be in the present and nothing else, a present which is the confrontation of what has been with what will be, a confrontation which results in the continuous creation of nothingness which thus becomes the very foundation of existence. If existence is the present, essence is the combination of existence past with the anticipation of what existence might be or should be ; anticipation which can only be constructed from what has already been and is eternally, since before being it had to be eternally possible so that the past is really the future of the Future. T. S. Eliot expressed that thought better though in a slightly different way.

Time present and time past
Are both perhaps present in time future,
And time future contained in time past.

The knowledge of the future or the knowledge of the essence of " tomorrow's existence " is an act of memory, it is an act by which the past continuously transforms existence into the knowledge of it and that becomes, in appearance, the ceaselessly changing essence of the being. Knowledge is the past recalled in the present but not the present itself ; one has to live in order to make knowledge possible, and " I think therefore I am " seems to me an impossible mental operation which should be replaced by " I think therefore I have been ", for when one thinks, existence is used as a means to make a nothingness which is part of the essence of life.

Valéry realized at the end of his life that to know is not to live, but on the contrary, to live is to know.   Incidentally those remarks seem to throw an interesting light on the penetrating insight of Wordsworth's ever incompletely quoted definition of poetry as " emotion recollected in tranquillity ".   We can see how an emotion recalled from the past is much richer than an emotion in the present, for emotions past become essences transformed, associated with others and receive the added impact of the present when the emotion is recalled.   That impact is also coloured by the aspirations towards the future, while the future of the time when the emotion took place has become the past recalled by the act of memory.   We have thus a complexity and a richness of mental associations and feelings which are the very stuff of poetry.

For Valéry believed in the freedom of the spirit.   For him the essence of man was to think, and then to create, or as Dante said in the " De Monarchia " : " To realize his powers of intellectual apprehension."   But, as Montesquieu and Lord Acton have emphasized that power corrupts and therefore needs to be limited, what is going to be the boundary to the ever-increasing power of the spirit which in its urge to reach its limits produces the discoveries and the instruments which destroy physical life and will end by reducing the spirit to the nothingness towards which it tends ?   Only a spiritual power can limit another spiritual power ; only faith in something supreme, beyond man, and thus beyond his spirit, can produce the necessary feeling of humility which will counterbalance the extraordinary power of the mind and prevent it from reaching the final absolute knowledge which will be the end of life.

The apparent unity of the Middle Ages, set up against a

background of intolerance, exploded into the religious wars which in their turn were followed by the scepticism of Montaigne and the acceptance of the established order which characterizes the seventeenth century. The eighteenth century, the age of enlightenment, is really the European century, the century of polished, refined manners, the century of Voltaire and Burke, the century in which from Paris to Moscow the same principles were accepted by the Court of Catherine the Great as well as by the Court of Louis XV. Valéry continues not only the seventeenth-century spirit but the age of Voltaire, sceptical and undogmatic, urbane, tolerant of all opinions, intolerant only of intolerance, the age which ended in the political intolerance of the Revolution and the exuberance of the Romantic period. Valéry is with T. S. Eliot the last of the neo-Classics. We are again living in an age of rising dogmatism and strong ideologies, an age of passions, political rather than religious, but even more dangerous because they seem to assume the intolerance of the Inquisition with greater force behind them. All sides claim to hold the truth, and those who believe in God claim to have Him on their side. The luxuriance of the Surrealist movement may have been our romantic explosion, yet Valéry is dead and his mantle lies on the ground. We should read once more d'Aubigné's best book "Les Tragiques"; it could be an apt and sufficiently strong warning against the dangers which beset us.

II

JULES SUPERVIELLE

SUPERVIELLE is with Villon and Verlaine the French poet who comes nearest to the accepted English idea of poetry. A spontaneous poet, greater than Verlaine, Supervielle is for the moment isolated in modern French poetry and is, with Valéry, with whom he makes a very interesting contrast, one of the most remarkable French poets of our time. In contrast with the scepticism of the former, Supervielle believes in everything; he believes in man, in Nature, in God, in life, which for him is not a kind of vacuum filled with the illusions of the intellect, but a constant source of poetic inspiration. For him everything is alive.

La lampe rêvait tout haut qu'elle était l'obscurité.

And the mystery of life is best penetrated when, as in dreams, Man, whose consciousness is abolished, lives the life of the Universe. That would seem to be a poetic attitude very near to that of the Surrealists. But Supervielle's visions, though never deprived of a certain air of mystery, are anything but obscure and his words are not born one from the other but are co-ordinated, following the poetic logic of an imagination which can penetrate everywhere and transform everything into a ceaseless metempsychosis of souls. If there is one French writer with whom Supervielle shows kinship, it is with Victor Hugo, the Victor Hugo of the " Contemplations ", the poet who wrote : " Ce que dit la bouche d'ombre ", a poem which is pervaded with that extraordinary pantheism which floats round the whole of Supervielle's poetry.

45

This pantheism is akin to the pantheism of Wordsworth or of Rousseau ; it is a feeling of oneness with Nature.

> Ta vitre connaît l'aube, et dit : Voir ! Croire ! Aimer !
> Les rideaux de ton lit frissonnent de tes songes,

says Victor Hugo. In both poets, animals and things seem to partake of Eternity and to know past and future. But for Victor Hugo man is time, a continuous beginning towards the future which he does not know but is striving to reach. For Supervielle man does not know the future but vaguely remembers the past. The fatality which weighs upon Nature is man's inescapable duty to seek God, and Victor Hugo says " Oui, ton fauve univers est le forçat de Dieu " :

> Les constellations, sombres lettres de feu,
> Sont les marques du bagne à l'épaule du monde. . . .
> Et sur cet amas d'ombre, et de crime, et de peine,
> Ce grand Ciel formidable est le scellé de Dieu.

thence the pity for the " Roi-forçat ", for man who is the prison of a restless soul. Like Orpheus, Supervielle constantly plunges into the underworld and tries to bring back to life all those broken parts which were once aggregated into living organisms and which have retained an inexpressible longing for life. The poet's constant concern is not with Death, an abstraction or a personification, but on the contrary with the Dead, with the loved human beings that have lost their human shape ; and those are images which, following the poet's words, anybody could conjure up and clothe with the emotions and sentiments which will give them life. As Victor Hugo says :

> Oh ! qui que vous soyez, pleurez sur ces misères !
> Pour Dieu seul, qui sait tout, elles sont nécessaires.

The difference between the two poets is, that for Victor Hugo everything which is below man, that is to say the animal, vegetable and the material, lives in pain, for it is the embodiment of past evils. For Victor Hugo creation is a kind of ladder with hell at the bottom, then the material, the vegetable and animal world, and towards the top are men and angels who are in touch with God. All those monsters are bound by fate to expiation. The tiger cannot help killing and the thorn cannot help pricking, and once upon a time the tiger had perhaps angel's wings and the thorn was perhaps a golden lock. The trees, the stones, havens of cursed souls, bemoan their fate but cannot change it ; consequently they deserve our pity. They wait dreaming of God, contemplating him, hoping for a future liberation, for suffering is not eternal and there are moments in time when a breath of love passes over that tormented world. Then all troubles and hatred are forgotten and the wolf is a brother to the lamb. The God of Victor Hugo is still Jehovah. For Supervielle, on the contrary, trees, flowers, animals, and stones are brothers of men, and they do not, as in Victor Hugo, contain the souls of those who did evil. In fact, in Supervielle the problem of evil is not faced. God is a kind of poet, full of compassion, deserving our love and pity, for he is just as bewildered as we are. Creation was for God a kind of gamble and he really does not know what is going to happen to it. Though Supervielle is far from having Victor Hugo's faith, he accepts God as a kind of equal who can give help, but who also needs it. His is not a God like the God of Victor Hugo who can embody Clytemnestra in a scorpion and Philip the Second in a pair of red hot pliers ; he is rather a God beset by problems which he cannot solve but a God full of love for man and for the universe in which men and things are at one in trying to solve or at least to shelve the insoluble problem of Death. The relationship of God and man is expressed in the most moving and one of the best poems of Supervielle called " Tristesse de Dieu ". No poet has discovered such pathos in the plight of God witnessing the harrowing experience of his dearest creation which he can no longer help.

Hommes, mes bien-aimés, je ne puis rien dans vos malheurs . . .
Je suis coupé de mon œuvre,
Ce qui est fini est lointain et s'éloigne chaque jour.
Quand la source descend du mont comment revenir là-dessus ? . . .

Et je vous vois avancer vers d'aveuglants précipices
Sans pouvoir vous les nommer, . . .

Homme, si je t'ai créé, c'est pour y voir un peu clair
Et pour vivre dans un corps, moi qui n'ai mains ni visage . . .

O mon enfant, mon chéri, ô courage de ton Dieu,
Mon fils qui t'en es allé courir le monde à ma place
A l'avant-garde de moi dans ton corps si vulnérable

Ayez pitié de votre Dieu qui n'a pas su vous rendre heureux,
Petites parcelles de moi, ô palpitantes étincelles,
Je ne vous offre qu'un brasier où vous retrouverez du feu . . .

If Supervielle's poetry does not show the triumphant certi-
tude of Claudel, it does not show either the cold scepticism
of Valéry who, in " Mon Faust ", reveals the extreme of
nihilism.   Supervielle's poetry is pregnant with the sense of
mystery, and the countless ties which unite the poet to the
invisible, together with his aspiration towards a reality beyond
the senses, make of him a man who is religious in the true
sense of the word.   He appears as a man who although he
does not have a definite faith, is in a state of faith in the
primal cause of all things, a man whose love of mankind
makes of him a truer Christian than many who do not forget
their weekly devotions.

If there is a genuine poet, a poet who has an extraordinary
power of conjuring up images, of seeing the most unexpected
associations, that poet is Supervielle.   He is continuously
assailed by various presences and essences ; the universe in
its infinite manifestations is constantly clamouring at the
gates of his soul and asking for life.   The poet is the centre
of the universe ; he has a most tender, brotherly sympathy
for everything which is in it.   In seeking for words, he is
seeking for that which will give the universe life.   But just
as he is humble, loving before Nature who begs life from

him and from Man, so he treats words with a kind of angelic
grace. He never bullies them or shouts at them ; he begs
them gently to come and make possible that supreme action,
by which man imitates God in the act of giving life.

> C'est beau d'avoir connu
> L'ombre sous le feuillage
> Et d'avoir senti l'âge
> Ramper sur le corps nu,
> Accompagné la peine
> Du sang noir dans nos veines
> Et doré son silence
> De l'étoile Patience,
> Et d'avoir tous ces mots
> Qui bougent dans la tête
> De choisir les moins beaux
> Pour leur faire un peu fête,
> D'avoir senti la vie
> Hâtive et mal aimée
> De l'avoir enfermée
> Dans cette poésie.
>   " Hommage à la Vie."

But here there is no self-assurance, no pride, no feeling
that God is with him, for or against some people or some
things. For Supervielle God is above good and evil, above
right and wrong, in a world in which these epithets have
no meaning. Here we are at the very source of thought
and action ; the world is new as at its birth, as it is in the
mind of the child who has no sense of ethical values and for
whom everything is pure. It is the purity of Christ who
realized the failings of creation, the unavoidable existence
of evil ; who came on earth and accepted death in his human
shape so as to transcend both good and evil ; who instead
of overcoming Satan, sought to absorb him into the whole,
into the undivided Godhead, which is absolutely good, where
evil has no place, for even hell is not eternal and will one
day cease to be. God having decided to break his Unity
and make creation possible, perhaps in order to know himself,

E

or simply to follow the compulsion of his own essence,
created at the same time Satan who is the symbol of the failing
inherent in creation.   But the failing is in creation, in the
Creator in Time and not in Eternity.   If creation had to be,
it could only be imperfect ; otherwise it would not have
happened, it would have remained God.   Perhaps tired of
eternity and non-being, God was driven to create, but it was
left to Christ in the shape of man to redeem creation by
refusing to take up the challenge of Satan, and by dying
to redeem Satan and to destroy the foundation of evil.   In
the world of Supervielle, nothing dies, there are only constant
metamorphoses.   The Universe rests on human thoughts :

> Et un nuage, un autre nuage,
> Composé d'humaines prières
> Se répandent en sourds ramages
> Sans parvenir à se défaire.
>> " Une étoile tire de l'arc."

Like Valéry he could say " l'homme pense, donc je suis,
dit l'Univers ".   Reality as we apprehend it, and reality
as it essentially is, become constantly fused into a single
intuition of eternity.

> Un chêne croyant à l'été
> Quand il n'est que l'âme d'un chêne
> Offre son écorce ancienne
> Au vent nu de l'éternité.
>> " Une étoile tire de l'arc."

.   .   .   .

> Et je doute si le boulevard
> N'est pas plus large que l'espace entre le Cygne et Bételgeuse
> Ah, si je colle l'oreille à l'immobile chaussée
> C'est l'horrible galop des mondes, la bataille des vertiges.
>> " 47, Boulevard Lannes."

Here we see the continuous process of relating the universe
to man, the constant interpenetration of one by the other in
a timeless world ; but in order to experience those feelings :

" il faut étouffer la mémoire qui pourrait faire du bruit ".
One must forget knowledge and just look and feel, and then
everything will always be new as in the first days of the
world, this world which lives through man—but the day will
come when :

> . . . la Terre ne sera
> Qu'un aveugle espace qui tourne.

Then only the essence will remain.

What is the world of Death ? It is a place where one sees
the creations of the world of the imagination, the place where
in spite of different appearances, all things are the same
because they are eternal. Thus the lion and the lamb, the
tiger and the child, can live side by side in a place where one
cannot die. What did the dawn of the world look like ?
Supervielle, the magician, can make those mysterious
moments come to life. In " Matin du Monde ", we have
the fascinating picture of a strange luxuriance and the simultaneity of the most unexpected things ; souls looking for
their bodies, the waves undecided, the stars forgetting to
shine, the simultaneity of past and future in the present, the
accepted order of things reversed. What are normally taken
to be the emanations of matter or the result of sensory action,
in brief the abstractions or the essences, exist before the
realities of the world. A neighing is looking for a horse,
a face is looking for a body, and looks are searching for eyes
in order that each may be given life.

> Regards sans iris et racines
> Rôdant dans l'espace argentin
> O regards, serez-vous enfin
> Retenus par une rétine ?

In " Equipages " we see that the essences exist at the same
time as these manifestations of the real world.

> Une jeune fille est assise, elle fait miroiter son cœur
> Comme un bijou plein de fièvre aux distantes pierreries.

In the very beautiful poem of "Houle" we see the perfect blend between Nature and Man,

> La terre est une quenouille que filent lune et soleil
> Et je suis un paysage échappé de ses fuseaux.

And the continuity of things, the oneness of life and of the universe

> Une vague de la mer naviguant depuis Homère
> Recherchant un beau rivage pour que bruissent trois mille ans.

Nothing dies, everything is there, present, whether past or future, and man's memory contains the world. For man lives and, though he dies, he knows the sweetness of hope and the fragrance of the rose ; but the stars are eternal, and their fate is to be always the same.

> Les étoiles restent seules contractées
> Au fond de leur fièvre
> Avec leur aveu dans la gorge
> Et l'horreur de ne pouvoir
> Imaginer une rose
> Dans leur mémoire qui brûle.
>   "Haut Ciel"—"Gravitations."

The trees, the stones, the stars, the sun, and the moon are part of life. Those who live and those who do not, those who change and those who do not, are necessary to one another. Time cannot live without the source of eternity, and the preference is for Time and not for Eternity, for everything that has lived wishes to go on living in any shape or form, even in illusions.

> Rien ne consent à mourir
> De ce qui connut le vivre
> Et le plus faible soupir
> Rêve encore qu'il soupire.
>   "Souffle"—"Gravitations."

Even the Dead, when the earth has been deserted by life and has become a lonely traveller of the sky, even the Dead will be sorrowful for the solitude of the Earth.

> Le ciel est effrayant de transparence,
> Le regard va si loin qu'il ne peut plus vous revenir

The sky will then be transparent, empty. Nothing will meet the look which will be lost in infinity, or the words which will never return ; and yet the eyes need other eyes to reflect their light, the self needs another self or other selves to echo its words, to make life possible, and man, lonely and bemused, stands at the centre of the universe. He is :

> La bougie qui éclaire le monde

witnessing events and omens which he does not understand, and he never knows if what comes to him has been or will be, or whether it is darkness or light.

> Tout ce qui mourut sur terre
> Rôde humant de loin la vie
> Interrogeant les ténèbres
> Où se développe l'oubli.

Life is the haunting thought of everything that has died. Dispersed into its essences, voices, ideas, dreams, affections, eyes, faces, through the ages irrespective of Time and Space, all that has been ever lingers round the windows and the doors of life hoping to enter it once again, to emerge from the nothingness of oblivion, and also from the eternity of the stars which, like everything else, hope that the human eye will bring them to life. And so we have whole villages,

> Village où l'âme faisait rage,
>
> Et qui ramassé sur la mer,
> Attendait une grande voile
> Pour voguer enfin vers la terre
> Où fument de calmes villages.

Everything is latent in the world of non-being, where there is no Time ; the world which belongs to the earth where smoke rises from the calm villages, and Time and Eternity meet as the village, " où l'âme faisait rage ", born from the waves of Eternity, comes to life on the shores of the earth. Nothing disappears.

> Un ruisseau de ma mémoire
> Reflétant un ciel confus ?
> .   .   .   .
>
> Compagnons d'un autre monde
> Pris vivants dans votre rêve
> Je vous regarde au travers
> D'une mémoire mouillée.
>   " Géologie "—" Gravitations."

We can, " à travers une mémoire mouillée " remember everything that has been, throughout the ages from the time when the heart was " salin sous la fable des eaux ", and even when we are dead it is impossible to forget what has been. " Je ne puis voyager qu'avec tous mes souvenirs ", and the " Forçat " of history remains present in the " Mémoire mouillée ", the memory of Eternity, performing the same gestures, fixed in the same attitudes. Eternity contains the past and the future, but the present, though naturally latent in Eternity, exists in Time.

> Je vais clandestinement du passé à l'avenir
> Parmi la vigne marine
> Qui éloigne du présent.
>   " Le Forçat Innocent."

Like most poets Supervielle can at times write bad poems, but these are singularly few. The short collection called " Poèmes de Guanamiru " is the one which seems to contain most of his bad poetry ; I mean poems such as " A Lautréamont " which Supervielle must like since he included it among his collected verse, or poems like " Equateur " and " Disparition ". Only the last poem in this group—" La

Terre "—seems to me to be really good. It shows the " Young Suns " looking askance at the ageing earth :

> Tu alimentes ton feu central de nos rêves les plus tremblants.
> Prends garde, tu ne seras bientôt qu'une vieillarde dans l'espace,

Beware that one day, man, with all that made life since the beginning, may desert you and settle down in other parts of the sky. Meantime the " Forçat " who is the dead, condemned to immobility, asks for news about the trees and the rivers :

> Ont-elles encore cette façon si personnelle
> De descendre dans la vallée,
> De retenir l'image de leur voyage

and he talks very movingly of man's condition as being :

> Comme l'eau d'un bidon qui coule dans le sable
> Et qui dans un instant ne sera plus que sable.
> "Le Forçat Innocent."

Man turns towards the stones, the friendly stones, whose hearts have just ceased to beat but who have known life, and remember things ; and he asks for their friendship. Here we have a poetry of pervading pantheism. Life is everywhere, mingled, intermingled, metamorphosed but continuous. Everything that has been continues to be in essences which surround us, in events which live in space, having been or about to be ; they can be detected by the supreme eye which ignores distances or time. Consciousness tries to apprehend events and sensations and tries with them to arrest time ; but that is not possible, nothing stays :

> Combien d'oiseaux perdus qui deviennent la rue,
> "Saisir."

In spite of the fact that we love our reminiscences, that we are unwilling to part with them, the day comes, when they must be laid to rest in the white room of Memory where

they become the image of Truth.   One tries in vain to seize
things, to stop life :

> Saisir enfin le jour
> Par la peau de son cou,
> Le tenir remuant
> Comme un lièvre vivant ?

But really everything slips away, thoughts and realities, so
let sleep seize us and transport us :

> Dans le bois de mille lieues
> Aux feuilles toutes baissées
> Comme paupières fermées.

This poem contains some of the most beautiful lines that
Supervielle has written :

> Grands yeux dans ce visage,
> Qui vous a placés là ?
>
> De quel vaisseau sans mâts
> Etes-vous l'équipage,
>
> Depuis quel abordage
> Attendez-vous ainsi
> Ouverts toute la nuit ?
>
> Feux noirs d'un bastingage
> Etonnés mais soumis
> A la loi des orages,
>
> Prisonniers des mirages,
> Quand sonnera minuit
>
> Baissez un peu les cils
> Pour reprendre courage.
>   " Saisir."

The pattern, the rhythm, the music, the beauty of the imagery
give to that short invocation an unforgettable beauty.

In Supervielle's poetry, as we have already seen, the senses,
the different parts of the body have a life of their own, the

hands dream of other hands, the heart in its cage, knowing
no difference between day and night, forgets, carried away
on the waves of desire, the memory of Death. The walls,
brothers to man, know the meaning of Love and feel in their
hard souls the presence of the loved one ; and men or stones,
pure essence or perennial pains, they all wait for something
which one day will awaken them to life. This life will be
complex, ever present, overlapping, difficult to seize in its
manifestations which are the symbols of a world beyond
the senses, a world of essences, just as :

> Cet arbre si proche, déjà ressemble
> A de beaux souvenirs remuant dans leurs cendres.
> > "Saisir."

For Supervielle the world is composed of elements and
particles, each having a life of its own, and at the same time
an awareness of its surroundings. Even the most integrated
living organism, like the human body, is a kind of universe
in miniature with veins for rivers and bones for mountains,
a whole world of separate entities, all living, questioning, and
wondering about their fate,

> Ah comment apaiser mes os dans leur misère,
> Troupe blafarde, aveugle, au visage calcaire,
> qui réclame la mort de son chef aux yeux bleus
> tournés vers le dehors ?
> > "Oloron-Sainte-Marie."

and realizing that men only love because they are part of a
whole. The dead with whom Supervielle holds the most
moving conversations, as with friends who are submitted
to a different tempo of living,

> O morts à la démarche dérobée,
> Que nous confondons toujours avec l'immobilité.

continue to be part of the world of being, their presence
continuously intermingled with our own. Yet outside Time

they are only possibilities which the living must bring to life. There is no realization except in the present, in the here and now.

That explains why, in the words of Blake, " Eternity is in love with the productions of time " and that belief places Supervielle in his age, the age of existentialism, whose main tenet is, that Eternity can only be grasped through Time in moments when Time, past and future, is transcended in the timeless present :

> Et pour rassembler les morts qu'une rumeur effarouche,
> Je suis le battant humain,
> Que ne révèle aucun bruit,
> De la cloche de la nuit.
>
> " Oloron-Sainte-Marie."

Hence those moving conversations among the Dead, anxious to know what the sun, the rivers, the human eyes are doing, for they cannot know except through the living who give them life. Hence that kind of silent union and solidarity between the dead and the living, between the countless component parts of the body which exist in harmony and are the constituents of life. Thus the eyes which see the world say to the bones, the brotherly bones :

> Et toi, rosaire d'os, colonne vertébrale,
> Que nulle main n'égrènera,
> Retarde notre heure ennemie,
> Prions pour le ruisseau de vie
> Qui se presse vers nos prunelles.
>
> " Oloron-Sainte-Marie "<br>" Le Forçat Innocent."

The burden which faces the living being is a heavy one. He not only has to maintain cohesion in his microcosmic universe so as to live, but he must also carry with him the life of the Dead, and sometimes that is too much. Why can the Dead not leave the living in peace ? Why can they not leave him alone when he is overwhelmed with so many responsibilities ?

> O morts, n'avez-vous pas encore appris à mourir. . . .
> Ne posez pas ainsi vos doigts sur le cœur des hommes
>   vivants. . . .
> Ne vous mélangez pas à nos pensées
>   Comme le sang frais aux bêtes blessées. . . .
> Laissez le fruit mûrir au fond de son loisir
> Et sans que le pourrisse un brusque repentir.

Let children live their dreams and life carry out its appointments.

> Dès le premier pigeon du jour jusqu'à la nuit noire de
>   loups.
>   " Supplique "—" Le Forçat Innocent."

At times the living are tempted to say : " Let us enjoy life without the burden of the dead " ; but the living never take long to realize that the qualms of the dead will soon be their own qualms, that they too will soon be begging life from humanity, so they are always ready to help the eyes which have been looking for a face through the ages, for they realize that there is not much difference between the living and the dead.

> Moi qui ne suis parmi les hommes
> Qu'un homme de plus ou de moins
> Tant le vivant ressemble au mort
> Et l'arbre à l'ombre qui le tient
> Et le jour, toujours poursuivi
> À la voleuse nuit.
>   " Les Yeux "—" Le Forçat Innocent."

One must note the word " voleuse " which indicates that the poet is far away from the " tempests " and " night " so dear to the Romantic age. He prefers day to night, joy to pain, if that is possible. Neither is Supervielle the poet of pessimism, nor despair, nor even doubt, the doubt which is so dear to Valéry. If we take " Sans Dieu ", one of the best poems from the " Forçat Innocent ", we shall see that Supervielle never loses hope. The sky through which he wanders, lost, is silent and unilluminated but he still maintains a certain optimism.

> J'avance entre les astres avec deux chiens aveugles
> Qui parfois se rapprochent pour chercher mon chemin.
> On ne voit rien ici qui ressemble à la Terre

He goes forward in spite of the briny scent, symbol of dissolution, in spite of the fact that he does not see anywhere " Les empreintes de Dieu ", in spite of his anxiety at being lost alive in the world of the Dead, a world in which he even doubts about the meaning of his memories.

> Terrestres souvenirs
> Qu'appelez-vous un arbre,
> La vague sur la plage,
> Un enfant endormi ?

yet a world in which he feels that he is not quite alone for

> Autour de moi les mains errantes des amis,
> Sentant que je suis seul égaré dans l'espace
> Me cherchent sans pouvoir trouver l'exacte place

But in spite of the solitude, in spite of the torments and what seems to be unavoidable, impending fate, the poet still maintains hope and goes forward.

> O ciel, ciel abaissé, je te touche des mains
> et m'enfonce voûté dans la céleste mine.

That poem also shows that although Supervielle has succeeded in conveying to the reader his philosophy of life, he does not do that by starting from an idea and then by trying to convince the reader of its value, but simply by describing poetic impressions. These have a truth of their own more penetrating and lasting than any didactic statement. In times when an important poet like Valéry was often giving the example of writing a poetry of ideas, or when poets like Claudel or Aragon were expounding their religious and political creeds, Supervielle stands out as the pure poet refusing to deal in anything but poetic impressions.

To the scepticism of Valéry or Proust about love, Supervielle, a man of flesh and blood, lover as well as poet and thinker, replies :

> Vivante ou morte, ô toi qui me connais si bien,
> Laisse-moi t'approcher à la façon des hommes.
>
> .   .   .   .
>
> Ah que j'arrête un jour ta chair à la dérive,
> Toi qui vas éludant mon désir et le tien,
> > "Le Forçat Innocent."

As for Supervielle's attitude to the self, it is not surprising that a poet who, like Blake, saw life in every atom and conceived the universe as composed of elements endowed with a life of their own, should have conceived the self as an element, changing to the point of non-recognition and worrying its envelope or its inmates with its continuous wanderings and with the fear that one day it might not return.

> Mon moi est loin, perdu dans quel voyage,
> Comment savoir même s'il rentrera.
>
> .   .   .   .   .   .
>
> Est-ce moi qui suis assis
> Sur le talus de la nuit ?
> Ce n'est pas même un ami.
> C'est n'importe qui.
> > "Réveils."

For, how is one not to be afraid, asks the poet, once the bones and the flesh are alone without the self ? And then there are all those selves waiting and hoping one day to live. He questions them without dogmatism and without any attempt to boast of a magic which he does not possess ;

on the contrary, he approaches them very humbly, as he
approaches everything, alive or dead, words included.

> Comment faut-il vous parler
> Comment puis-je vous toucher
> Ne pouvant vous approcher ?
> "Ruptures"—"Le Forçat Innocent."

For it is so difficult to know what is the self, in a world in
which everything overlaps, continues, changes. The faces
which one sees, have they surged from the living memory,
are they centuries old, reminiscences of other times, and other
shapes, or are we living among the symbols and signs of
the real world which lies beyond the mountains and the plains
of human life ? Who knows ? Supervielle asks the question,
but does not attempt to answer it. He leaves that to the
reader ; yet sometimes, as he says, he is terribly alone.

> Je suis si seul que je ne reconnais plus la forme exacte
>   de mes mains
> Et je sens mon cœur en moi comme une douleur
>   étrangère.

It was noted previously that Supervielle follows the main
trends of the thought of his time, including some of the tenets
of the existentialist philosophy.

A line like : " Je suis resté vivant dans la glu de la nuit "
could be taken to mean that he, as an individual, detaches
himself from the elements, the *glu* of non-being and lives by
his will, by his desire to live and to be. This short poem
which follows reminds one of a striking phrase in one of
Sartre's plays " L'enfer c'est les autres ".

> Dans votre propre cœur
> Entendez vous le pas
> Mais c'est plutôt la voix
> D'une femme qui pleure
> Dans la chair sans issue.
> A peine elle remue
> Pour ne pas effrayer
> Son malheureux geôlier.

But, on the other hand, for Supervielle the world is one.

Man is not, as the existentialist believes, surrounded by a universe of things which he uses as a kind of " viscosity " which he transcends in the awareness of his existence, in his attempt to realize his self, the self which projects him forward towards " Le creux toujours futur " of Valéry. For Supervielle, though the essences can only really live through man in Time, they exist as possibilities ; they commingle in the most unexpected relationships.

> La distance et les poissons
> Mélangés à l'eau de mer
> Tissent des illusions
> Que surveillent les éclairs
> Dans la nuit sous-marine.
> D'obscures tentations
> Veulent former un matin
> Que nul regard n'a glané.
>   " Le Forçat Innocent."

It is only in man that nature really lives, but man and nature are friendly, nature is not " une ' marâtre ' ou ' une tombe ' ". Because she is centred on man and is part of a life that could not be without her, man is always ready to lend his heart to bring out the feelings of nature, and his eyes to reflect them. This is beautifully expressed in the poem " Echanges ".

> Un chêne ne savait,
> Et ne pouvait un orme,
> Une pierre n'osait,
> Hésitait une roche
> Un fleuve allait toujours
> Moins fort que son désir
> Mais ils se retrouvèrent
> Dans le feu d'une lèvre
> Dans le cours d'un regard
>
>   .   .   .   .   .
>
> Et la pierre eut des glands
> Et l'orme des poissons
> Et l'étoile filante
> Refusa de filer.

Here we note the word " feu " which seems to indicate that
for Supervielle, as for Yeats, it is only in the fire of passion
that the eternal moment and the absolute Oneness of all
things can be realized.

The emergence of life from the chaos of non-being is not
easy, there is so much to forget.

> Il me faut mettre de l'ordre
> Parmi toutes ces étoiles
> Que je vais abandonner.
> Au fond d'un sommeil sans bornes,
> Il me faut me dépêcher.

So says " L'enfant née depuis peu " who cannot decide any
more whether she still is part of the sea, loch, or river, and
who cannot discover the secret of her flesh.

With Supervielle it is difficult not to yield to the temptation
of quoting too much.   Not only is his poetry remarkable for
its sustained high standard but one is always stumbling across
passages which one has not the heart to leave unmentioned.
How could one omit the beautiful lines which begin the poem
" Le Pommier " :

> A force de mourir et de n'en dire rien
> Vous aviez fait un jour jaillir, sans y songer,
> Un grand pommier en fleurs au milieu de l'hiver.
> > " Les Amis Inconnus."

or the moving beauty of " Figures ", the poignant thought
that without knowing how and why the circle around oneself
shrinks and changes.

> Je bats comme des cartes
> Malgré moi, des visages,
> Et tous, ils me sont chers.
> Parfois l'un tombe à terre
> Et j'ai beau le chercher
> La carte a disparu.
> Je n'en sais rien de plus.
> C'était un beau visage,
> Pourtant, je l'aimais bien.

Je bats les autres cartes.
L'inquiet de ma chambre,
Je veux dire mon cœur,
Continue à brûler
Mais non pour cette carte,
Qu'une autre a remplacée.
C'est un nouveau visage,
Le jeu reste complet
Mais toujours mutilé.
C'est tout ce que je sais,
Nul n'en sait davantage.

"Les Amis Inconnus."

And if one wants to breathe an air of apocalypse, to be led through lands where everything shakes and shudders in the wake of the spirit or of some prophet, read the poem "Le Hors-venu".

Quand ils passaient, même les arbres
Étaient pris de vivacité,

Les troncs frissonnaient dans la fibre,
Visiblement réfléchissaient.

And the name of the "Hors-venu" was

"Plus-grave-que-l'homme
Et-savant-comme-certains-morts
Qui-n'ont-jamais-pu-s'endormir."

Nobody has depicted better than Supervielle the pity of Death. Malherbe, and Maynard, Baudelaire, and certain Romantic writers had depicted the starkness, the horror, the macabre of Death. For Supervielle the Dead is a brother who has lost the means to feel the warmth of the sun, the radiance of light and the comfort of human affection; he is what we shall be, what we have been; we shall plead, as he does, for human faces to reflect our dead thoughts, for human ears to hear our words, weighed with gravity and lasting wisdom. Supervielle has supremely the gift of pity.

F

Le monde est plein de voix qui perdirent visage
Et tournent nuit et jour pour en demander un.

Je ne sais plus mon nom, je n'ai plus de cervelle
Et ne puis disposer que de celle des autres.

C'est beaucoup d'approcher une oreille vivante
Pour quelqu'un comme moi qui ne suis presque plus.

and in another poem he says :

Il n'est plus grande douleur
Que ne plus pouvoir souffrir
Et que l'âme soit sans gîte
Devant des portes fermées.

When he was only eight months old, Supervielle lost both his father and mother. It is hardly worth while stressing the capital importance of such tragedies in life, particularly in the life of a very sensitive being. To find oneself with nothing at one's back, or rootless like a spectral tree, is a terrifying experience. Supervielle endured it, and all his life he tried to liberate himself from the obsession of the past, which for him was the void, and from the fear of tomorrow. Because of his experience of the past, fear was the only form of knowledge he had. One has only to read the very moving poem " Portrait "—" Gravitations " to realize his plight :

J'ai été toi si fortement, moi qui le suis si faiblement,
Et si rivés tous les deux que nous eussions dû mourir
    ensemble, . . .

The shadow of death weighs over most of his early poetry. This is no romantic attitude but something inherent in him and probably due to his early isolation. Life was for a time the expectation of death but he succeeded in mastering that obsession. He conquered it by seeing in the poet a medium whose function it is to keep alive the dead and he visualized death as the means to regain some sparks of the Heraclitan fire.

We have seen how those problems of solitude and death have been finally mastered ; we have seen how the poet felt

not only alone, but, that within himself, all was solitude.
The limbs and the body are isolated from the soul, the various
selves are isolated and continuously changing, and God himself is alone, more lonely than anybody else—yet in the end
love can conquer solitude and the fear of night and of death.

Tossed about between his two motherlands, France and
Uruguay, Supervielle spent a great deal of his time sailing
the Atlantic, travelling between the one and the other. That
" Ulysses of Montevideo ", as he calls himself, must have
spent months, perhaps years, at sea in the course of his
numerous voyages, and his poetry echoes with the distant
murmur of waves, and throbs with their mysterious life.
The monotony of the sea, its impression of immensity, are the
same as that of the pampas, which for Supervielle is another
kind of sea. Both convey the same impression of infinity
and of a kind of novelty reminiscent of the dawn of the world.
Supervielle's poetry rises from that context where things,
animals and men have not been forced together into niches
and social conventions which have dwarfed them. His world
is the world of wide horizons. His vision reaches to the
distances where sand or water meet the sky. It is from his
early life spent with Gauchos in the pampas that Supervielle
derives his love and knowledge of beasts. No poet conveys
better than Supervielle the primitive grandeur which characterizes the life of the Gauchos, no poet has been more
fascinated by horses and cows and described them with the
same profound sympathy :

> Les bêtes n'ont jamais une plainte bruyante
> Et portent leur douleur comme l'arbre son fruit.

In his poetry there is room for all the animals which he
has loved in his youth and still loves ; in fact, we find ourselves in an atmosphere in which all men, Christians or Non-
Christians and all animals live happily together as at the very
beginning of life. The earth becomes a very insignificant
thing in the vast universe which contains it, and man regains
his place amongst the animals, who are as important as he is.

We are back to the lost unity, and if we were able to journey through the forests of our souls we should discover inhabitants who are our brothers :

Dès que nous sommeillons tout devient animal,

says Supervielle. The animals are with the poet and live with him :

Les tremblants animaux de la création
Vivent dans le canal étroit de mes artères.

Before concluding this brief study on Supervielle, one should perhaps say a few words about the problem of " influences " and the problem of creation and poetic diction.

The search for influences in the work of a poet may be a fascinating game, but it is fraught with dangers and it is not, on the whole, very rewarding. In the end the true poet finds in others only what is latent in himself. We all know the debt which Baudelaire owed to Poe (and now we may add the debt which Poe owes to Baudelaire), but in the end Baudelaire had to be Baudelaire in order to find what he found in Poe's work, which to no mean extent is what he put into it. Supervielle has taken care in the course of interviews to disclaim any affiliation with the recognized schools of poetry —Symbolist or Surrealist—while at the same time confessing his admiration for certain exponents of both. " There is in me something opposed to Surrealism, it is the urge to communicate, . . . poetry must not be a crossword puzzle ; mystery must be its perfume and its reward." " . . . The masters to whom I owe most ? I am so afraid to forget certain names that I prefer not to quote any ; and my debt is not confined to writers only, it extends to painters, musicians, architects, to the countries which I have visited, to the faces which I have seen, and to the hands which I have shaken. . . . I should be greatly embarrassed if I had to decide whether I owed more to Homer or to the liners which ply the Atlantic between Bordeaux and Montevideo."

Unperturbed by the attempts made by some poets to find

a new diction, to discover new fields of vision, or, like Aragon, to introduce new techniques, Supervielle finds in poetry his natural, genuine medium of expression. He has no set purpose, he does not try to unfold patterns of rhyme and alliteration which, however effective, seem forced. He accepts the rhyme, the half rhymes and assonances. He very often, as in his latest poems, confines himself to the traditional forms of French poetry, but he is at ease in any form, and what stands supreme for him is the poetry which makes its own natural form. " I believe that the poet may make use of the classical type of verse or of other types of verse according to the rhythms of his emotions, but I think that the *verset* and the blank verse are better suited than other forms to convey the complexity and rhythms of modern life." Rhythm is for Supervielle the most important thing, and it can, according to him, produce a kind of æsthetic beauty which before was only obtained by the discipline of very strict forms. We have stressed earlier Supervielle's delicate approach to words. We must add here one more remark on that subject, and it is that the words which he seems to love most are the humble, everyday words, with the one single exception of adjectives ending in " euse ", a sound which is soft and melodious, leaving behind a kind of prolonged echo.

When dealing with the problem of poetic creation, one cannot do better than allow the poet himself to give us his views. This is what Supervielle said in an article which appeared in the " N.R.F." : " Inspiration is for me the feeling that I am everywhere at the same time, in space as well as in the various recesses of the heart and the mind. The poetic state creates in my mind a kind of magic confusion, during which ideas and images become alive, leaving their places either in order to connect with other images—in that world all things are close—or to undergo profound metamorphoses, which render them unrecognizable. For the mind immersed in dreams, contraries no longer exist, affirmation and negation fuse into one single thing, it is the same with past and future, hope and despair, madness and reason, death and life. At that moment rises the internal song, which chooses the appropriate words. And I witness all those things, interfering as little as possible and being dimly aware of impressions which normally should be contradictory. I meet my Self, I get lost, I frighten and reassure myself, I liberate and entangle myself, I give myself life or I kill myself. I give myself the illusion of helping the obscure in its effort towards the light, while on the page appear the images which from the depth stirred and moved towards life. After that I know better what I am, where I am ; I have created dangerous forces, I have exorcized them, I have transformed them into allies of my inner self."

Further on we find in the same article a phrase which sums up Supervielle's attitude towards Surrealism. " I have always refused to write poetry for the specialists of mystery. I feel rather humiliated when a normally sensitive being does not understand one of my poems ; I say to myself that it must be my fault, and I turn it on all sides to try to find out where the flaw lies." There we have modesty together with the assertion of a genuine desire to speak to one's fellow-beings.

Of all the contemporary French poets, Supervielle is certainly the one who possesses in the highest degree the gift which makes the poet—imagination. Supervielle's imagination is not the visionary imagination of Blake, Victor Hugo, or Rimbaud, but the kind of pervading, ever-creating imagination which sees life in everything, which embraces the cosmos and which can clothe every *démarche* of the mind or of the heart into creations and suggestions apprehensible by the senses. The inexpressible is conveyed in symbols, images, or metaphors, which arouse awareness of another world, a world of plants and animals, a world pivoted on man and throbbing with his heart and pulse.

III

PAUL CLAUDEL [1]

CLAUDEL'S philosophy is contained in his "Art Poétique" and "Connaissance de l'Est". In "Cinq Grandes Odes" he tried to convey through the medium of poetry what he had expounded in these two books. The first ode "Les Muses" precedes his "Art Poétique" and is an anticipation of it. Claudel expressed through that poem his conception of poetry; the poet sings because he has to; the poet, appointed instrument of Providence, divine vessel, becomes at times so filled with inspiration, that he bursts out:

> Faisant sauter la clôture, le souffle de lui-même
> Violentant les mâchoires coupantes
> Le frémissant Novénaire avec un cri !
>   "Les Muses"—"Cinq Grandes Odes."

There in a powerful image with the very word "novénaire" which stands both for the nine muses, and for the nine months of the period of human gestation, and other meanings too, Claudel conveys the force and the inevitability of the poetic creation. Mnémosyne, or "Memory", is the first of the Muses, the store of the imagination, the silent one, and yet the foundation of poetry, the very link between Being and Non-Being, between Time and Eternity which memory mysteriously recalls. From the memory there arise literary associations of voyagers and poets, from Ulysses to Dante; but Claudel will not follow the pattern of Dante who was guided

---

[1] Paul Claudel is first and foremost a poet-dramatist, one of the greatest of our times; I hope to devote a special study to this aspect of his genius.

by Virgil and Beatrice ; he wants no pattern, he wants no
guide, he wants to wait for the inspiration :

> O mon âme, il ne faut concerter aucun plan ! o mon
> âme sauvage, il faut nous tenir libres et prêts,

and Claudel explains his conception of poetry :

> O grammairien dans mes vers ! Ne cherche point le chemin,
> cherche le centre ! mesure, comprends l'espace compris entre ces
> feux solitaires !
> Que je ne sache point ce que je dis ! que je sois une note en travail !
> que je sois anéanti dans mon mouvement ! (rien que la petite pression
> de la main pour gouverner).
>
> Ainsi un poème n'est point comme un sac de mots, il n'est point
> seulement
> Ces choses qu'il signifie, mais il est lui-même un signe, un acte
> imaginaire, créant
> Le temps nécessaire à sa résolution,

and before this Claudel had said :

> O mon âme ! le poème n'est point fait de ces lettres que je plante
> comme des clous, mais du blanc qui reste sur le papier.

The poet listens to silence and transcribes the song which
he hears, or as Rimbaud did, tries to convey the visions which
he sees, and the poet does that with the words : " In the
beginning was the Word ". In " Paradise Lost " Adam, at
the request of the Archangel, gives human names to creation ;
he does that in the age of innocence when he is still in perfect communion with his Creator, and thus his words probably echo on the human plane the words of God. The
poet, who can find again the original meaning of words,
brings back to existence the things which he names and thus
repeats the action of God who created with the Word. The
poet's joy is to discover the right name for everything :

> Mais comme le Dieu saint a inventé chaque chose, ta joie est dans
> la possession de son nom,

Et comme il a dit dans le silence " *Qu'elle soit !* ", c'est ainsi que,
pleine d'amour, tu répètes, selon qu'il l'a appelée,
Comme un petit enfant qui épelle " *Qu'elle est* ".
O servante de Dieu, pleine de grâce !
Tu l'approuves substantiellement, tu contemples chaque chose
dans ton cœur, de chaque chose tu cherches *comment la dire* !
Quand Il composait l'Univers, quand Il disposait avec beauté le
Jeu, quand Il déclanchait l'énorme cérémonie,
Quelque chose de nous avec lui, voyant tout, se réjouissant dans
son œuvre,

" Les Muses."

That " quelque chose de nous " is memory, which vaguely
remembers the creation, when we were all present, which
was the eternal present containing everything, and from which
God was bringing the world out of Non-Being by the instrument of His Word. In the same way if one can remember
the original name of things, things cannot fail to come to life
at the call of the poet who, speaking in the name of God,
reveals things to themselves :

Que mon vers ne soit rien d'esclave ! mais tel que l'aigle marin qui
s'est jeté sur un grand poisson,
Et l'on ne voit rien qu'un éclatant tourbillon d'ailes et d'éclabousse-
ment de l'écume !

That image is a cruel image, an image of violence, and yet
it does describe the nature of Claudel's poetic creativity which
indeed consists in pouncing on ideas and images which are
lurking in the dark or in the half light, and in trying to
bring them to full daylight. The result of that attitude is
that very often one sees no picture except disorderly movements and flashes of the struggle ; one hears no music, except
vague exclamations or half uttered words which are the echoes
of the effort. What a difference from Supervielle who gently
coaxes everything, words and ideas ; who would never com-
pare the poet to a fierce eagle pouncing on a fish caught
unaware and unprepared for such an unwarranted attack.
It is difficult not to be slightly repelled by such a picture of

violence. Here in the midst of ceaseless movement which becomes at times disorder, and like somebody who fears the dizziness of the heights, the poet asks the *muse modératrice* to hold his hand while he continues to bend over the abyss.

Un poème . . . est lui-même un signe, un acte imaginaire créant le temps nécessaire à sa résolution.

O poète, je ne dirai point que tu reçois de la nature aucune leçon, c'est toi qui lui imposes ton ordre.

In fact, sometimes one should not talk of Claudel's poetry, but of Claudel's ideas and emotions expressed in poetic prose for there is no metre, although there is a certain rhythm, the rhythm which one finds in any prose, when the tenseness of the emotion rouses the writer to a rhythmical expression. As for cohesion, selectivity, these are often lacking : the poet is carried away by his visions, his emotions, and he does not attempt to make his images, however potent they may be, congruent to the theme. The end of " Les Muses " is strongly reminiscent of some of Mésa's words to Ysé in " Partage de Midi ".

In the next ode, " L'Esprit et l'Eau ", the analogy between water and spirit, though complex, is not difficult to see in its main lines. Both elements are pervading, dissolving or binding ; the spirit is the very source of life, the water is the primal element, from which human life has evolved. The spirit returns to God just as all the waters return to the sea and originate from the sea. Both spirit and sea are symbols of liberation, and what the poet is longing for, is liberation, but liberation in God.

O mon Dieu, mon être soupire vers le vôtre !
Délivrez-moi de moi-même ! délivrez l'être de la condition !
Je suis libre, délivrez-moi de la liberté !
Je vois bien des manières de ne pas être, mais il n'y a qu'une manière seule
D'être, qui est d'être en vous, qui est vous-même !

God is the end of man, and the world is the way to God and everything in the world reflects God and the spirit which binds it together.

Claudel is not, like the Romantics, tired of life (at least in his poetry) and ready to welcome death as a deliverance ; he welcomes death as a means to return to God whom he asks to free him from Time. God is the end of man, says Claudel, but man is the end of God. It is not for nothing that Claudel quotes constantly the prophets and the Bible ; he is a mystic and his vision, merging into God, becomes God's vision.

Salut donc, ô monde nouveau à mes yeux, ô monde maintenant total ! . . .

J'ai pesé le soleil ainsi qu'un gros mouton que deux hommes forts suspendent à une perche entre leurs épaules.

J'ai recensé l'armée des Cieux et j'en ai dressé état, . . .

" Les deux hommes forts " ; one is Claudel, the other is difficult to find. It might stand for the symbol of God. Claudel too believes that everything partakes of Eternity ; he sees the leaf falter and die, but the leaf which the poet describes in his verse does not perish, it is independent of Time.

Et moi qui fais les choses éternelles avec ma voix, faites que je sois tout entier
Cette voix, une parole totalement intelligible !

And the poet asks to be liberated from matter, so as to return to the Essence, for he says :

Je ne mourrai pas, mais je suis immortel !

" Let me cease being obscure," says Claudel, " make use of me." He comes near asking to be the *logos*, the word of God. At least he asks for sainthood, and that overwhelming desire to merge into God is perhaps formulated with too great a force and only reaches its adequate expression in the end when he says : " O ami, je ne suis point un homme ni une femme, je suis l'amour qui est au-dessus de toute parole."

That is St. Francis. Claudel ends in that attitude of humility after having realized with great sorrow that he is separate from God because he, too, has sinned.

> Et moi aussi, je l'ai donc trouvée à la fin, la mort qu'il me fallait ! J'ai connu cette femme. J'ai connu la mort de la femme.
> J'ai possédé l'interdiction.

The last lines of the ode are filled with repentance and humility, and renewed echoes of " Partage de Midi ".

Life for Claudel is a continuous metamorphosis. He believes in the separation between spirit and matter, the body and the soul, and seeks liberation from the body and union with God for he suffers from being deprived of his presence. Union with God seems to be an eternal Nirvana, the past being completely forgotten. " Que je ne retourne pas à la vie des hommes," says Claudel. One cannot help thinking of Supervielle and his love of man, Supervielle in whose poetry even God wants to be amongst men. For Claudel eternity seems to lie in the word,

> Qu'il ne reste plus rien de moi que la voix seule.

and the word is the only way to God and to the mystical experience.

> La voici donc au seuil de ma maison la Parole qui est comme une jeune fille éternelle.

He is always in a high state of exaltation. Yet neither the prophets nor the Cumaean were possessed by God, nor by the gods, all the time ; they had moments of respite.

Claudel is a belated Romantic. His poetry is very egocentric ; he is more than often directly concerned with himself or with his relation with God, and he is led to an exuberance of feeling which is not redeemed by any moderation in expression. Instead of the " objective correlative " which enables T. S. Eliot to be as personal as Claudel, or the whole symbolization of the " Divina Commedia " which enables Dante to do what every writer does and can only do, that is to speak about himself, Claudel does so directly, without intermediary, and thus, often, his poetic statement becomes mere rhetoric, loaded no doubt with images of extraordinary power, but still eloquence, and not poetry.

" C'est moi," says the sea, " je tire, j'appelle sur toutes mes racines, le Gange, le Mississipi." Because of his Orphic way of writing, his poetry is marred by disappointing lapses and lack of taste. He talks of " Le Nil avec sa double vessie ", of " La matrone Lune " ; he indulges in a pun which though congruent to the meaning remains nevertheless a poor pun.

La matière première ! C'est la mère, je dis, qu'il me faut !

Not only is this out of place, but presented in that rather colloquial form, it has strange connotations.

In " Magnificat " all those private conversations with God, all those exultations about the poet's renunciation of the world, his impatience of Time, his lack of interest in the perfume of the rose, leave the reader unimpressed. Here we have a supposedly mystical experience which is described with a great wealth of detail and with a vigour of voice testifying that the poet is anything but overwhelmed by the experience. As for the belief that the intensity of this outpouring is enough to create the rhythm, that the poet can dispense completely with form, and the resulting verses be called poetry, that seems to me rather difficult to accept. It is not indeed the number of feet, nor the rhythm, nor the rhyme, which make the poem. But while rhyme can easily be dispensed with, even with advantage, not so rhythm. The verses for example of Shakespeare and Milton on the whole are not rhymed but they certainly have definite rhythm and metre. The rhythm is thus extremely orthodox, easily varied with trochaic or dactylic feet when required, and yet unmistakable and impossible to forget. With Claudel the rhythm rarely follows any of the accepted patterns ; it is the rhythm of his breathing which is obviously subject to his passion or to his rather rare lack of passion. But ideas, thoughts, and emotions which move Claudel deeply do not necessarily move the reader to the same degree, and he watches in amazement the poet's gesticulations and excitement while he himself remains cold and disconcerted. After all, passions, sentiments, and beliefs are purely a matter of temperament. Some are stirred by the sight of mountains or of the sea, which leaves others unmoved ; some are roused by beliefs which others find repellent. Although it is not necessary to share the poet's beliefs (cf. Dante and Milton), we do expect something more from him than a highly emotional statement of his beliefs. If for want of recognizable rhythms we could have what one might call a rhythm of images congruent to the main theme, pivoted on a centre or born from a central fire (cf. the poetry of Dylan Thomas), then the magic would work and the poem rise from the page and enter the soul and memory of the reader. But Claudel's images, though at times extremely potent and vivid, are not selected with sufficient care to make of the poem an entity. The reader is dragged at high speed, to the accompaniment of Apocalyptic sounds, over mountains and vales and at times through the starry heavens ; but although he may be exhilarated by this kind of dazzling experience, in the end he finds himself on the hard earth, exhausted and bewildered.

This poem throws an interesting light on the poet's attitude towards God who is for him the God of wrath, who condemns *les infâmes* and the unbelievers, the God from whom the poet could borrow thunder and lightning in order to destroy the unfaithful and the impure. It is the God of d'Aubigné who said in his poem " A Dieu " :

> Veux-tu longtemps laisser en cette terre ronde
> Régner ton ennemi ? N'es-tu Seigneur du monde . . .
> Les moineaux ont leurs nids, leurs nids les hirondelles ;
> On dresse quelque fuie aux simples colombelles ;
> Tout est mis à l'abri par le soin des mortels ;
> Et Dieu seul, immortel, n'a logis ni autels.

and Claudel says : " Ne me perdez point avec les Voltaire, et les Renan et les Michelet et les Hugo et tous les autres infâmes ! Leur âme est avec les chiens morts, leurs livres sont joints au fumier."

"La Muse qui est la Grâce" is perhaps the most didactic of Claudel's poems ; it is the best exposition of Claudel's poetic conception. Claudel begins by trying to describe the coming of poetic inspiration. The beginning is like the beginning of "L'Esprit et l'Eau" :

Hors de moi la nuit, et en moi la fusée de la force nocturne, et le vin de la Gloire, et le mal de ce cœur trop plein ! . . .

Ah, je suis ivre ! ah, je suis livré au dieu ! j'entends une voix en moi et la mesure qui s'accélère, le mouvement de la joie, . . .

O muse . . . puisque . . . je suis un peu ivre en sorte qu'un mot parfois
Vient à la place du vrai,

It is a force beyond the poet's control which invades him, and makes of him a different being, not "un être maudit" as Baudelaire or Rimbaud would have it, or a man condemned to suffering as Byron or Chateaubriand described the poet, but an "elect" of God born to sing His praise, and to praise His creation. But the error of Claudel is to think that inspiration would dictate to him the words which could not fail to be poetry. There are times when that is so, but there are other moments when inspiration is a bad counsellor. Here we have the struggle, between the muse who demands his constant allegiance, and the poet who wants to remain a man. He offers to write the poems of the earth.

Le grand poème de l'homme enfin par delà les causes secondes réconcilié aux forces éternelles,
La grande Voie triomphale au travers de la Terre.

The poet should sing the achievements of man, and record the life of mankind, but it should be a record of man's life free from hazard, that is to say, free from the reason that produced knowledge. The Muse or Inspiration is highly indignant at the poet's submissiveness to Reason which cannot save him from Death. Only Inspiration, the source of Eternity, can do that, but Inspiration free, uncontrolled, like the Pythoness or the Bacchantes. It is not Reason, the instrument of knowledge, which transforms the world, but, on the contrary, Imagination.

> . . . suffit de le regarder seulement, de ces deux yeux de l'esprit qui voit et qui entend.

The Muse, like the God of Claudel, will not accept any compromise ; those who seek her must follow her everywhere, blindly, without hesitation. The poet resists, he wants to remain amongst men, all he wants is to contemplate for a moment that face which destroys death.

> . . . mon devoir n'est pas de m'en aller, ni d'être ailleurs . . .
> Ni de vaincre, mais de resister.

And the poet clings to the earth and refuses to listen to the voice which might convince him ; but in the end he must listen to it, for it is the voice of inspiration which enables him to exercise his art which is revelation. The Muse refuses to give him up and contrasts the beauty of flames with that of stones which are solid :

> Que parles-tu de fondation ? la pierre seule n'est pas une fondation, la flamme aussi est une fondation.

The stones are submitted to the law of gravitation, the flame rises towards heaven, the poet very nearly yields for he realizes that inspiration is the voice of his Source,

> O idée de moi-même qui étais avant moi !

and there follows what is probably the expression of the very essence of Claudel's poetic creed. In order to hear the voice of the Muse or to receive the divine grace which enables him to create, to make the world live with his word, the poet must accept the death of his self.

> O passion de la Parole ! ô retrait ! ô terrible solitude ! ô séparation de tous les hommes !

He must leave all men in order to exercise the gift of God which is the revelation of the invisible world through the visible world by the Word.

> Et moi c'est le monde tout entier qu'il me faut conduire à sa fin avec une hécatombe de paroles !

The finality of the world is to be expressed in words ; in order to do that he must liberate himself, he must die in order to be born :

> O libérateur des hommes ! ô réunisseur
>   d'images et de cités !
> Libère-toi toi-même ! Réunisseur de tous
>   les hommes, réunis-toi toi-même !
>
> .   .   .   .   .
>
> Comme la parole a tiré toutes choses du néant,
>   afin qu'elles meurent,

He will thus see the great mystery of the sun burning out what he has created.

And the poet in the middle of that holocaust sings the praise of the spirit, but he is not ready to be carried away for he hears a voice, an earthly voice—

> J'entends mon antique sœur des ténèbres qui remonte une autre fois vers moi,

—and the poem closes on that most moving note describing the unresolved conflict between flesh and spirit, between the human being and its higher aspirations.

To sum up, we might say that creation in Claudel is a painful experience, as when the Pythoness is invaded by the god. The poet, he says, must cease to be himself, he must give life in pain, he must create the world with words out of himself. The poet is a demiurge and Claudel seems to believe as some thinkers do, that as God's essence was bound to evolve into creation so also for the poet creation is a necessity from which he cannot escape. The poet indeed is the sufferer possessed by the god who does not leave him

G

until he has spoken through him.   One cannot think of a
more Orphic conception of poetry.

> Ce n'est point toi qui m'as choisie,
> c'est moi qui t'ai choisi avant que tu ne sois né.
>
> Pourquoi Dieu ne serait-il pas libre comme
> toi ? Ta liberté est l'image de la sienne.

But of course one absolute freedom excludes another unless
there is a covenant.   The poet, like the " elect ", has been
chosen, for what reason we do not know, to be the voice
of the Muse or the voice of God.   He has no alternative but
to submit himself to being the instrument of Providence.
That Claudel finds the task congenial and delights in being
the prophet is beyond doubt, but one cannot help feeling
that that ineluctable Fate which for religious or artistic reasons
weighs on certain men is a conception more native to the
Old Testament than to the New.   The human creature is
given no option, free will is out of the question and there
is no attempt to persuade him of the greatness of his task.
He is simply invaded by God, amid flashes of lightning and
roars of thunder ; a very apocalyptic scene.   Or he is pounced
upon as the fish or the innocent lamb is pounced upon
by the bird or the beast of prey, and after a brief pathetic
struggle he must submit to the will of fate and to force.
Furthermore, he must become its mouthpiece.   Let it be said
that all our sympathies are for the fish and for the lamb,
and that no thunder can shake man, puny animal that he is,
out of the conviction that he is greater in his suffering and
annihilation than the terrible force which overwhelms him.
We are far from the extraordinarily humane atmosphere of
Supervielle, or the pervading love of St. Francis, from a
world in which everything, everybody is patient, and where
God prevails by persuasion and man is not overthrown by
force ; a world of no absolutes in which God himself, the
supreme power, at times wonders about the fate of man
and worries about the creation whose love he needs, as a
father needs his children's love ; a world where there are no

" elect " amongst children who are all equal and are judged
by their behaviour, and where those who most generously
illustrate the divine principle of " Love ", are held up as
examples to the others. But it must be love of everything
and above all love of one's neighbour ; not an exclusive love
between God and one who is supposed to be his elect. Such
an interpretation of Love would probably exclude from the
Kingdom of God all those who are inflamed with burning
zeal and who wield the thunder of divine wrath against their
fellow-beings.

Je n'ai aucun soucis que vous aimiez ou non ma parole . . .
mon désir est d'être le rassembleur de la terre de Dieu,

says Claudel. What the poet asks from God is the grace
to speak convincing words and to bring God into every heart.
But again we must stress the fact that the God of Claudel is
a God before whom the human creature is filled not only
with love but also with fear.

Faites que je sois comme un semeur de solitude et que celui qui
entend ma parole,
Rentre chez lui inquiet et lourd.

Not only is knowledge, according to Claudel, impossible
without God—" tu ne peux connaître qu'avec Dieu en toi ",
but his poetic imagination is closely associated with his faith
and becomes at times the record of his religious and mystical
experience.

Voici qu'avec cette mèche de quatre sous, j'ai allumé autour de
moi toutes les étoiles qui font à votre présence une garde inextin-
guible.

In reading Claudel it is sometimes difficult to repress a
slight feeling of irritation, and this is undoubtedly due to
the obtrusiveness of belief unredeemed by the magic of poetry.
Listening to, or reading " Paradise Lost " one is never intent
on weighing the philosophical and metaphysical ideas of
Milton, an attitude which would preclude poetic enjoyment,

but on the contrary one is completely carried away by the greatness of the poetry in a world in which belief and disbelief are held in suspense. The poetry which underlies Satan's creation, which is born from the poet and bears no doubt the hallmark of its creator, is sufficiently objective or indirect to stand apart from the poet as a living poetic creation. That is even truer of Dante's " Divine Comedy ", in spite of the fact that the cosmological and religious beliefs which we encounter in Dante are even more remote from us than those which we encounter in Milton. But in Dante's great poem, a poem in which curiously enough the poet is the centre, the object, the catalytic agent for the whole, the element which reflects all thoughts, lights, and emotions from Heaven to Hell, from God to Satan, the poetry seems to reach greater heights than Milton's ; for here indeed the whole cosmos, God and angels, remains a kind of grandiose mystery and only lives as it is refracted by the poet. God retains His majesty beyond words in silence, and Hell speaks through hundreds of human voices. To associate Claudel with such poets as Dante or Milton is not to infer that he is comparable to either of them, but simply that he raises in a more than acute form the problem of belief in poetry. In Claudel the statement of belief remains direct, personal, burning with conviction and sincerity ; but one must remember that sincerity unadorned by the grace of music and by the magic of poetic transmutation is anything but poetry. It can provide strangely incongruous images like " L'Astronome épiant avec la même poignante curiosité le visage de Mars qu'une coquette qui étudie son miroir," or " le premier souffle de la mousson d'été pareil à une femme suante et nue ". What seems at times to mar this poetry is the pride of the man who has the right faith and is then assured of eternity, and the pride of the poet who can play the demiurge. In spite of appearances and a great deal of Christian symbolism and ritual there seems to be a singular lack of humility, of humanity, of spontaneous love for the living and above all for the dead, a love which cannot be replaced by timely

prayers and masses. Here we find once more the note of
stark realism which characterizes great Catholic writers from
Malherbe to Baudelaire ; here we see death in its cruel form,
and the living do a great deal of rationalizing before they
pay the dead the attention which they deserve, and that
attention is sometimes nothing more than a yearly ritual.
There seems to be no bliss in Claudel's world of the Dead,
but on the contrary suffering until the coming of the Kingdom
of God. Of course, Claudel needs his human brothers, but he
wants to be amongst them " le semeur de silence, le semeur
de ténèbres, le semeur d'églises, le semeur de la mesure de
Dieu ". There must be silence to hear God's voice, darkness
of the senses so that only the soul can see and point the way,
and every man must contribute to the building of the Church
of God.

The greatest poetry of Claudel seems to me to be his
dramatic poetry, for in the drama what is sometimes a serious
defect in his lyrical verse, that is to say his over-intensity,
becomes objectified. In " L'Annonce faite à Marie " which
is a real *mystère* of the Middle Ages, an extraordinarily moving
liturgical drama, the tenseness is unrelieved from beginning
to end ; this produces the atmosphere of overwhelming
pathos which grips us at the realization that the road to God
is a difficult road, that the ways of God are mysterious and
awe-inspiring. Faith pervades everything. From the very
beginning, when the father, impelled by a mysterious voice,
decides to break up this happy home and set the wheel
moving, we feel everywhere the hand of God, the veil of
predestination, and a strange conflict takes place in us. We
are torn between our admiration for the purity and greatness
of the Saint, and our profound sympathy for the being who
has been chosen to bear the most harrowing mental and
physical pain in order to assert the ways of God to man.
We realize how difficult, how superhuman it is to be a saint
and we cannot help echoing at times a phrase of Mara who
seems to be no more responsible for her wickedness than
Violaine is for her sainthood.

"J'honore Dieu, mais qu'il reste où il est." God seems to be the jealous God who watches over his creatures and reminds them of his presence by wrecking what seemed to be well-established happiness, happiness which can only exist through rebirth. It is the conflict between the human and the superhuman as it takes place in Violaine which is extremely moving, and makes of " L'Annonce Faite à Marie " what is probably a great play, in which the characterization of the *dramatis personæ* is expressed in moving poetry. Indeed, those who are at times puzzled by the play must never forget that it is a poetic drama and not a prose drama, a drama full of symbolical meanings in which the statement is hardly ever direct. Drama enables Claudel to avoid some of the pitfalls of the ideal which he had set himself ; the ideal of being the man of God, God's voice ; the ideal which is responsible for a certain fixity of attitude which is on the whole opposed to poetry. Indeed, Claudel's creative process seem to me to show a certain violence, and a certain forceful-ness which are in contrast with the generally accepted attitude of expectancy and patient groping which has been that of the most outstanding poets when writing under the spell of " inspiration ". It does show a certain fixity due to the existence of an ideal which the poet has chosen and to which he wishes to remain unswervingly faithful.

After his conversion Claudel seemed to have felt more and more as the man of God, as being one of God's voices, therefore the quality of " negative capability ", that quality " of being in uncertainties, mysteries, and doubts, without any irritable reaching after fact and reason " which, as Keats pointed out, Shakespeare " possessed enormously ", seems to have progressively disappeared from Claudel's life. He ceased to be the chameleon poet, the poet who could say with Keats " when I am in a room with People if I ever am free from speculating on creations of my own brain, then not myself goes home to myself ; but the identity of every one in the room begins so to press upon me that I am in a very little time annihilated—not only among Men ;

it would be the same in a Nursery of children . . ."
("Letters", I, p. 245). He became the prophet, the Man
of God, co-ordinating the poet's feelings from the outside
and not allowing the feelings and sensations to co-ordinate
themselves and to unfold with ever-renewed freshness along
the unbroken ever-changing flow of consciousness which
illuminates and grows more and more powerful so as to
reach the recesses of the unconscious mind. Claudel knew
probably too well where he was going and what he was
doing. Once he had experienced his illumination on the
Road to Damascus, he forgot too completely the doubts of
St. Paul, of St. Augustine, or the sensuous mysticism of
St. John of the Cross, and his poetry suffered.

Indeed, it seems to me that these remarks will assume their
full value if one applies them to one of Claudel's earliest and
possibly greatest play, " Partage de Midi ". In that play
which is one of the two or three most important poetic
dramas of our time, Claudel, though touched by the light of
God's grace, still retains the violence and pride of the pagan.
The play which is one of the most moving and one of the
most lyrical plays ever written, owes a great deal of its pathos
to the conflict between the beliefs and the uncertainties of
the main protagonists, between the awareness of sin and the
overwhelming desire to plunge into it, between the knowledge of God's love and God's will and the deadly urge to
transgress them, swept away by the feeling that absolute
possession of the being which belongs to God can only be
achieved through death. Ysé knows her incompleteness and
knows that in spite of her passion, or perhaps because of
her passion, there exists an ineffable state which human love,
physical or spiritual, cannot create. Only in death can she
reach that absolute, and so she wills consciously her death
and that of her lover in an attempt to fulfil themselves in
the face of God, in an apotheosis of pagan grandeur and
yet still trusting in God's mercy to sanction their love in
eternity.

The lyrical sweep of the verse matches the tense pathos of

the emotions and makes of the play a remarkable poetic drama. In that play the characters have, on the whole, lives of their own. We do not have the feeling of supernatural intervention. In spite of what Claudel says in his preface, " in order to take man away from himself, to enable him to have the knowledge of *the other*, . . . there is only one appropriate instrument, the woman ", in spite of that claim of Claudelian dogmatism, that dogmatism that God makes use of certain human beings as vessels of his will, is not apparent here. It is true indeed that Mésa is a man who has had his revelation on the Road to Damascus, without having become fit to be admitted into God's bosom, because he retains his human pride and the arrogance of his purity, without the awareness of sin and thus without the possibility of God's grace, so that the woman is the instrument with which God will break him, will bring him to Him through sin and humility. One can feel that, and one can say that the play would have been mechanical if the central character of the play, Ysé, had been all of a piece, a single-minded instrument of divine providence as Violaine for instance. But on the contrary Ysé is until the end a real human being, unpredictable, uncontrollable, a force of nature and a force which can only manifest itself through and by other beings which become part of the pattern of life, whom in the end she drags down with her to catastrophe.

Life is constant movement, and the drama is the artistic creation which is, like life, constantly moving. In the drama the poet can express all his feelings and all the various aspects of poetry from the lyrical to the didactic and the epic, and when the dramatist is a great poet, when he is successful as Shakespeare is in his greatest creations, the result is that the plays are first and foremost poems. " Hamlet ", like " King Lear " or " The Tempest ", is a great poem in which several forms of poetry find expression through the different characters. Like every vital heart and mind, these character experience certain emotions all of which reflect an aspect of the artist's personality.

Claudel is undoubtedly a poet of great gifts. His plays are certainly poetry and on the whole they are more successful than his purely lyrical poems. The distinction between lyrical and dramatic poetry is perhaps an artificial one. Among the " Grandes Odes ", for instance, the " Muse et la Grâce " has certain passages which can properly be called dramatic. But the dramatic form is superior to any other form of literature in its revelation of the human soul. Knowledge is, above all, delimitation, and that implies, points of contact with other souls and interactions between them ; these are not only more revealing than any introspection, but are the necessary complements to it.

It is not difficult to find in Claudel's works examples of bad poetry, of sheer rhetoric, grandiloquent, pompous and interspersed with gross errors of taste. A poem like " Tant que vous voudrez mon général ", which undoubtedly expressed the genuine patriotism of Claudel, is a good illustration of these failings. It was probably written in the fire of inspiration and faith which swept France to victory in 1918 ; but it does stand as a convincing example that the noblest feelings, patriotism or any other, are not in themselves poetic material which can be used directly without transmutation. One cannot help thinking of the sober, yet how moving, preface of Wilfred Owen's war poems : " This book is not about heroes, deeds or lands, glory, honour. . . . My subject is war, and the pity of war,' and unforgettable poems like " Greater Love ", " Exposure ", " Mental Cases ", and others come to mind and imprint upon the heart the pity of war. Here we are in another world, a world which is both harrowing and human, remote from the enthusiasm of Rupert Brooke, or the " élan " of Claudel. Claudel's thought of thanking Christ and the Holy Virgin for having saved France is a noble thought but it remains utterly unchristian. It is just as unchristian as the prayer of ministers asking God to give us victory over what we call our enemies, who obviously address to Him the same prayer. Here, once more, the remarkable words of Wilfred Owen in one of his letters come to mind : " Christ is literally in ' No Man's Land '. There men often hear His voice : Greater love hath no man than this, that a man lay down his life for his friends. Is it spoken in English only and French ? I do not believe so. Thus you see how pure Christianity will not fit in with pure patriotism." War is a savage mental aspect of man's character, and the poet whose main qualities are imagination and sympathy with his fellow beings, if he deals with the theme of war, best fulfils his task when he tries to awaken in his readers an intense pity for the sufferings of men, and when he tries to alleviate by his words the miseries of humanity. Both Wilfred Owen and Siegfried Sassoon are undoubtedly among the finest of war poets because they saw only " the pity of war " and because they applied their poetic imaginations to the interpretation of some of the most moving themes and situations which are to be found in human life. Yet Claudel too can be very moving. The second poem in the volume " Poèmes et Paroles " is certainly a moving and remarkable poem which expresses both the horror and the pity of war. It comes as near as possible to great poetry for it combines lyricism and inspiration with form.

" Pater Noster " is on the whole a good poem with what seems to me a slight blemish at the end, the introduction of a carnal element in an emotion which is completely spiritual. It does indeed complete the picture of the woman's emotional background, but somehow the poem would have been on a higher plane if it had remained in its incompleteness. Every masterpiece is in some sense incomplete, since it raises more questions than it can answer. " Aux Martyrs Espagnols " is a poem full of invective against the enemies of the Nationalist cause. " Prière à la Vierge " and " St. Martin " are good poems, while " Cinq Grandes Odes " are the most important lyrical poems that Claudel has ever written.

For Claudel, everyone, everything is related to the whole universe and to its creator. One has the feeling that in Claudel the way to happiness and joy is through pain, and that happiness is not for this world. In order to find God

we have to renounce ourselves and the ways of the world
and the pain lies in the remembrance as well as in the physical
suffering which can be transcended by the belief that this life
is really a mere transitional stage. In "L'Annonce faite à
Marie" the Christ-like sacrifice of Violaine unites the family
and brings peace to its members. Violence is among the
traits of Claudel's early works, and in the war poems he
finds the confirmation of the faith in sacrifice which exists in
man.

For Claudel all roads lead to Rome, the centre of truth
and beauty. "Le Protestant prie seul, mais le Catholique
prie dans la Communion de l'Eglise," says Claudel in "Le
Soulier de Satin". The Protestant is incomplete and, according to Claudel, is at a disadvantage in his attempt "to find
God's grace" and to be amongst the elect. But there is no
end to human pride, and Protestants, Catholics and all who
claim an exclusive possession of the truth share in that
pride which is not only the original but the fundamental
sin of man so well described by Blake in "The Everlasting
Gospel".

Symbolism has tried to give poetry the same range as
music and to restore the incantatory value of words. Claudel
is to a certain extent a symbolist and his admiration for Baudelaire and Rimbaud rests on a profound sympathy with their
aims and with their poetic methods.

"Les choses visibles sont faites pour nous amener à la connaissance des choses invisibles", said Claudel in "La Catastrophe d'Igitur". Claudel believes that that truth, that
invisible world which the word can bring back to life, exists
and is God's creation which the poet simply rediscovers. His
spiritual father is Rimbaud, and that is less extraordinary
than some critics seem to believe.

The Word has for Claudel the same incantatory power as
it has for Rimbaud:

Croirez-vous que je sois puissant à fouler ma grande vendange
de paroles,
Sans que les fumées m'en montent au cerveau.

In the process of creation he gets drunk with the words. The words must first of all by their music and prosodic arrangement create the trance-like state which annihilates the mind, and leaves the place free for the song of the soul. Then the words, free from their ordinary meanings, recover their primitive power of creation. Claudel attached great importance to the word or sign and therefore to the typography of poetry.

For Claudel there is not only the rhythm of the heart and the arteries, but also the rhythm of the thought which comes and goes and is not continuous but interspersed with blanks. Claudel's verse is above all the breath of his thought ; each thought spans his verse or verses. One can easily see the arbitrariness of such an assertion ; one thought can expand into a page just as fireworks can blaze into a thousand stars. But, above all, there is no common denominator between the thought processes of the poet and those of the reader, and there is no musical phrase shared by both which would guide the poem from its source to its rebirth in the reader's mind. So Claudel's assertion that the music of the words can lull the mind into a state of hypnosis, which will permit the process of this rebirth, is not always verified in his poetry. On the contrary, the mind is often kept awake by the attempt which it has to make to follow the poet's abstruse reasoning. Besides, there is no awareness of blanks between one thought and another when the mind is in a state of consciousness, and when it is in a state of subconsciousness no expression is possible, at least there is no awareness of it. Thoughts have no rhythm except the rhythm of their expression shaped by the emotions which govern them. Emotions are as varied in their manifestations as the individuals whom they affect, and unless a bare minimum of convention is accepted they are bound to remain essentially private and incommunicable. Claudel has written poems and ballads in which he has used traditional metres, but he is generally governed by the movement of the emotion which stirs him. Yet the Bible is there to prove that some of the greatest poetry has rhythm but no definite metre, and in the end all distinctions between poetry and prose are really arbitrary. Is there, for instance, more poetry in Voiture or in Pascal and Bossuet who wrote in prose, and are not the prose poems óf Rimbaud and Baudelaire greater poetry than some of the " perfect" verses of the Parnassians ? Claudel has a powerful imagination, probably the most powerful that has been at work in French literature since Victor Hugo, and imagination is what makes the poet. " Imagination ", said Blake, " is spiritual sensation," and Blake knew what imagination was. Keats, in one of his extraordinarily intuitive insights, came as near as possible to giving a meaning to the word imagination when he said, " The genius of poetry must work out its own salvation in a man ; it cannot be matured by law and precept but by sensations and watchfulness in itself. That which is creative must create itself." Nobody doubts Claudel's genius, and Keats' definition of imagination fairly accounts for the originality of Claudel's creations.

IV

A POET OF THE CHRISTIAN MYTH—
PIERRE EMMANUEL

TOGETHER with Claudel there are some other poets whose central symbols and myths are those of Christianity. Through Baudelaire, Rimbaud, and Victor Hugo they go back to the Old and the New Testaments. Like Baudelaire, they are preoccupied with the idea of original sin and breathe an atmosphere of strong spirituality which aims at raising man from the dust where he lies and at giving him faith in the future. At the same time those poets, strongly influenced by Baudelaire and Rimbaud, believe in the importance of the subconscious as a source of poetry; the " Correspondances " of Baudelaire are not only the mysterious links between various manifestations of nature, but also allegories and symbols of an invisible world which the poet must try to reach. Pierre Jean Jouve is the most important of those poets, and the younger poets who belong to the same group acknowledge their debt to him. But as his reputation is well established and as there have been already many studies of his poetry, the present writer feels that he cannot contribute anything new to what has already been said and he will simply confine his remarks to a poet who because of his youth, is far from having given the measure of his talents and seems to be the most promising of the young French poets; that poet is Pierre Emmanuel. There are two other poets who belong to this group, they are Patrice de la Tour du Pin and Jean Cayrol. Patrice de la Tour du Pin has just published an important volume of poems entitled " Une Somme de poésie ". That volume has been the source of various interpretations by the critics who nevertheless agree on the importance of de la Tour du Pin as a poet. Yet he is near enough to Emmanuel with whom he shares in the search for the Eternal beyond human reach, so that it seems to me not unwise to leave the study of his poetry to other critics and to say a few words about a lesser-known poet, of the same group, Jean Cayrol. Jean Cayrol has just published a volume of poems called " Larmes Publiques " which bears the traces of his harrowing experiences in German concentration camps. Christ and the Cross are the central themes of his poetry. Christ, eternal, living, and dying in each man, in each moment of a man's life, and submitted to the lowest forms of torture to enable him to rise to greater heights. There is probably no other time in history which calls more than our own for the symbol of Christ. Millions of men have suffered to death, watched by hangmen or by countless Pontius Pilates who washed their hands of the blood of their fellow-beings ; never has Christ's myth been more actual, more present than in our epoch, when man has become his own executioner upon whom Christ's forgiveness needs to be and is infinite. Jean Cayrol has lived the night in the olive groves, has witnessed the end of many of his friends who, comforted by the thought of the One who has been there before them, have all accepted the sacrifice of blood and fire with the calm confidence of men who already see the rising dawn. Their sacrifice has taken on a kind of ritual aspect, a kind of supreme Holy Mass on the threshold of a new world. The flames of those sombre fires and cremations which defaced Europe, were also the flames of the undying spirit which gives the eternal life, the blood was the blood of the eternal victim for the sins of man. Jean Gruber, an Austrian priest, can say with supreme poignancy and sublime beauty :

> Il est une heure, j'arriverai avant Jésus au Ciel,
> Ecce Venio, Mon Dieu j'ai devancé votre Fils,
> J'ai les pieds boueux mais les lèvres blanches de miel.

He accepts everything as necessary and he knows that flames do not destroy but transform. These poems are amongst the most moving of the war and Jean Cayrol is a poet whose remarkable imagination and keen sensitiveness make us look to him with hopes of greater achievements.

Pierre Emmanuel is the most important of France's younger poets. Like Claudel or Victor Hugo, Emmanuel is the poet of cosmic and apocalyptic visions and his biblical imagination lifts him towards the metaphysical heights whence he seeks to discover the future and to disclose it to his fellow-beings. Death haunts his thoughts, but beyond Death, on the horizon rises the pure image of Christ who brings man back to the Divine. "Tombeau d'Orphée" is, for the time being, in spite of its difficulties and obscurities, Emmanuel's most accomplished poem. The poem is an Orphic interpretation of creation which centres round the problem of sex. Sex is both creation and death, it is the source of Orpheus's suffering who will only achieve liberation by the death of sex. The only birth is the one which comes from Christ. Euridyce can only bear life and return to life by Christ, and the pure poet is born from Christ and divine inspiration, Christ who was born not through love of man and woman ;

> . . . substance aimée
> secrétée par la basse et reculante lèvre
> et déposée sédiment blond sur la statue
> d'une femme aux traits grossiers suant l'oubli
> sous les vents d'Est dont les harpes échevelées
> la poussent vers le mur d'atroces destinées
> bâti de lacérantes mains et de dents fauves
> la Mer.

If Orpheus could get rid of the memory of Euridyce, the dead woman living in him, which makes of him man and woman, being and non-being, he would get rid of death ; he carries with him the infinite present which is the nothingness of Euridyce and he can only live by trying to be that nothingness which in fact cannot be :

Mais quiconque un seul instant peut subsister dans une telle absence de soi-même est éternel.

H

Orpheus lives the agony of sex and dies because of it through
the unsatisfied passions of the Mænads. Orpheus longs for
Euridyce, at the same time the idea of sin inherent in the
woman is always present in his mind ; he knows that sex
is death, and thus he repudiates Eurydice in order to live in
Christ, and he asks God to liberate him from his duality so
as to be one in Him.

> Seigneur, quand déchirant ma double identité
> Tu m'absoudras de cette chair qui me tourmente
> Et Tu me donneras d'être homme devant Toi.

Orpheus becomes the symbol of the very life of the cosmos ;
like Tiresias he is at the same time man and woman, living
and dead, as the poet he is the consciousness of existence, and
after long hesitations he ends in rejecting Eurydice and chooses
to remain dead and to leave her dead so that being sexless and
sinless he might be integrated into the very principle of Life.

> Et tantôt jetés l'un vers l'autre la nuit
> tantôt se violant eux-mêmes en male rage
> ces deux êtres formaient un Etre de péché
> paisible, entouré d'arbres immobiles
> tout résolu en claire identité.

Eurydice has the same attitude to life and sin as Orpheus.
She prefers to remain happy in God rather than to return to
life with Orpheus who mistakes his own desire for her voice.

> Dieu m'aime
> Et me veut seule en Lui
> Ne reviens pas
> Ton chant te trompe
> Si tu crois.entendre ma voix

Supreme beauty apprehended intuitively cannot be expressed
in words and a tear, or tears are perhaps the only way of
expressing the inexpressible, and one cannot fail to note how
near Valéry Emmanuel sometimes is. " La Jeune Parque ",
overwhelmed by her fate, does not find any words to express
the disorder of her soul ; a tear is the only sign of her anguish.

In " Tombeau d'Orphée " we find such lines as " Toute beauté n'est qu'une attente comblée " which recall Valéry.

> Patience, patience,
> Patience dans l'azur !
> Chaque atome de silence
> Est la chance d'un fruit mûr !

But Emmanuel presses to a conclusion, which is that for him after having grasped the supreme expected beauty, death is the necessary inevitable end ; this is something very different from the conclusions that Valéry reached at the end of his life.

Contrary to what certain critics seem to think, Emmanuel does not take sides against Valéry's " Narcissism " or against pure idealism. Valéry realized more clearly than anybody else the danger of absolute knowledge based on self-contemplation and would have subscribed to :

> . . . le néant
> est le prix du plaisir cruel de se connaître
> et la lame ne peut se connaître qu'en tuant.

The thought contained in the above lines reaches not only towards Valéry but also towards Dostoievski, and as for the contention that the poem might be taken to mean the failure of idealism, that contention seems to me to be the very opposite of what appears to be the attitude of Orpheus and of the poet himself, which is that existence implying the suffering of sex and ultimately nothingness, it is best to remain in the state of non-being, the state of perfect possibility, part of the supreme essence which is God ; and the symbol of the tree, undivided, rejoicing in God and in its oneness, is also the poet and is one of the most moving of Emmanuel's symbols.

> . . . Aimeras-tu jamais
> assez pour comprendre l'audace de cet arbre
> enfin pur du tourment d'être seul, et grandi
> par le tacite éloignement du ciel d'automne
> jusqu'à se mirer nu dans le regard de dieu ?

The land where Orpheus lives is a land of solitude. The poet must be alone like a tree in the desert, in an atmosphere in which the layman or *le voyageur* breathes with difficulty.

> Oseras-tu le regarder—le temps d'un souffle—
> Et respirer la solitude entre vous deux

It is not against Narcissism that Emmanuel speaks, but against the division of man into male and female, and the ideal state for him is the state of oneness, the sexless, angelic state. The poet knows the meaning of life, the real life, while our world is only a desert. He alone can lead man to the gates of Eternity. For Orpheus, hell is the division into man and woman and yet as nothingness is part of existence and will end with it :

> Et jusque dans ma chair traqué par le non-être,

in the same way, he can only reach the Elysian fields by going through hell which is the woman

> . . . le secret de la femme et de l'eau c'est que l'eau
> n'est jamais lasse d'être femme, que la femme
> a de l'eau la perfide et fluide ubiquité.

> . . . il ne sait pas
> que la barque et le fleuve-femme ne font qu'un
> et que le sexe est naufragé en ses eaux noires.

" ' Qu'il ose marcher sur les eaux ', dit le démon." The poet or man cannot walk over the waters, he must swim or use a boat, he needs the woman to help him to bear the weight of his oppressing fate.

> Une femme s'ouvrant étrange sur les astres
> découpe une ogive de rêve dans le temps
> le captif s'y accoude et chante : de la tour
> qui le retient aux confins nus et militaires
> où contre l'Ombre est retranché tout le réel
> sa voix monte plainte éternelle d'Eurydice
> elle déchire de ses eaux vives les déserts
> elle console un ciel prostré chargé de chaînes
> son appel de palmes lointaines rafraîchit
> les bourreaux que toujours plus de terreur assiège
> d'un délire de murs de donjons et de nuit.

But Orpheus cannot escape his fate. Eurydice's memory is everywhere, he cannot free himself from her presence, and yet he can never grasp her and so she becomes his hell

> Il sait pourtant
> que seulement ici est la vraie morte : ici
> le cœur, le sceau qu'il faut briser pour que la Femme
> soit délivrée de lui, son seul Enfer.   Ah fuir
> ce sang qui bat au rythme atroce de la morte
> cette chair saturée de gestes anciens !
> Eurydice la trop absente trop présente
> il la crie morte hors de lui sauvagement
> et traînant son plaisir de cadavre en cadavre
> il n'en finit jamais de la ressusciter.

A beautiful passage showing that the poet is unable to exorcize his obsessing love.

The poem ends with the association of the poet with Christ or rather with the merging of Orpheus into Christ.   Three days the poet remains before rising from the dead.   The transposition takes place by using and by applying to Orpheus all the attributes and imagery associated with Christ, the wounds, the thorns, St. Veronica, the shroud, the spear, the face covered with blood and in the end the assertion that the pure poet is born from Christ.

> Le corps roulé dans le granit d'un autre corps.
> .   .   .   .
> Lui, rejetant le lin des morts gravit l'aurore
> et marche vers la Chair promise à l'Orient.

" Tombeau d'Orphée " could be considered as the conclusion of " Le Poète et son Christ " which is the first volume of verse published by Emmanuel.   " Le Poète et son Christ " contains most of the themes which are the foundation of Emmanuel's poetic experience.   Resurrections and artistic creations are generally preceded by a journey through Hell. Before creating, the poet must face the agonies which

Rimbaud faced, the attempt to grapple with the most obscure turmoils of the subconscious in order to find the symbols which enable communication, universalization through language. Before rising from the Dead, Christ must endure the agony of Hell which is neither the world of the dead nor the world of the living, but the in-between, with its harrowing memories and desperate hopes. Christ or " Lazarus " is also the Orpheus in search of his soul of " Tombeau d'Orphée" or the sinner of the " Sodome " of life, the one who understands that he is the living sin, the torturer of Christ. " Le Poète et son Christ " would be sufficient to place Emmanuel among the important poets of our time. There we find poetry of a very high order and of moving intensity. There, in a language which can combine the creative force of that of prophets and visionary poets, together with the subtlety of some of the great symbolical writers, we discover a poet who dares to grapple with the most moving and living symbol of human life—Christ. Most of the themes of " Le Poète et son Christ " are drawn from the Bible, but Emmanuel sees them as a man of the twentieth century, who has seen the world torn by wars, who has watched the greater and greater suffering of Christ in man overwhelmed by Satan. The poem " Golgotha " contains the central theme of the book, which is that Christ is as old as the world, and that man is the cross upon which Christ is crucified. Christ having assumed the shape of man has also assumed sin, and so man must long for Christ and suffer and die to hasten the liberation of Christ.

> Je meurs infiniment de Son péché je suis
> le rachat de la ténébreuse faute du seigneur
> je pleure mon dieu mort et veux pécher sans fin
> pour être le bois éternel où l'Amour saigne.

Original sin, according to the extraordinarily sensuous and moving poem " Madeleine ", is the sin of sex, sex which offers a strange and quasi-incompatible duality, for it is at the same time the foundation of life and creation which contains it, and the source of the death of consciousness, and, consciousness being Time, sex appears as self-destructive. It is Madeleine, sinner and saint, who until the end of Time gives birth to Christ.

> et la Sainte pâmée sans fin dans la vendange
> ose enfanter le Christ une éternelle fois
> ose Le refouler en son ventre de femme
> et Le mûrir ève gravide infiniment.

Every man is both Christ and the Cross, every man re-enacts in himself the symbol of the life of mankind which dimly re-enacts the great drama.

The poetry of " Le Poète et son Christ " is on the whole of a very high standard. From the Rilkean pantheism of " Lazare Ressuscitant " to the very moving poems of " Gethsémani " or " La Femme Adultère " the poet can express all the moving misery of man and his hopes. " La Femme Adultère " shows how Emmanuel can transform the material which he uses. The bare parable of the Bible which leads to the famous words " Let those without sin cast the first stone " has been clothed into images of extraordinary luxuriance which are tense with emotion and pathos. It becomes a brief but moving drama in the course of which we see the woman who yielded to the " jet sauvage du soleil " pursued by the mob imbued with the teachings of Moses and the respect for the Law, until she comes to the divine Judge who has come, not to condemn, but to love.

Those who describe, with reason, Emmanuel as a Christian poet would do well to meditate what kind of Christianity he preaches. Good and Evil are for him inseparable in Time. Satan is necessary to Christ.

> La sécheresse grince et tourne sur son axe
> Broyant Christ et démon en un même destin,

and those who wonder what is the attitude of Emmanuel

towards the Church and faith, a faith ever questioned, should read the passage

> O Pierre
> Eglise dévastée malgré tes saints
> porte à jamais murée porte à jamais ouverte
> Enfer et Ciel à deux battants ! Que tu es vaine
> fausse mort écrasant Christ sous tes raisons
> pierre fidèle jusque dans la trahison
> Epouse de l'Enfer et du Christ tout ensemble
> Mère jalouse plus qu'une louve, à la fin
> ôtée de ce tombeau

and the passage

> O Christ privé de mort voudrait mourir
> mais éternelle est l'agonie : jamais le vide
> n'est assez pur
> jamais l'explosion de vie n'est assez forte
> jamais le Christ n'est assez seul pour oublier
> le Fils de l'Homme.

Christ is part of man, He cannot rid himself of the burden of the Incarnation, and He cannot return to eternity as long as man of flesh and blood lives.

The volumes of poems like " Combats avec tes Défenseurs ", " La Liberté Guide nos Pas ", and " Jour de Colère ", which on the whole have been inspired by the events which the poet has witnessed and the chaos which he foresees, are part of the spiritual quest of the poet of " Le Poète et son Christ " and of the drama through which he lives. Christ is again the central theme, Christ throughout the ages. " Jour de Colère " seems to be less interesting than the other two volumes, which contain good poetry of a very moving and prophetic quality. In " Combats avec tes Défenseurs " the symbol of Christ is clear : He alone contains both the sufferings and the hopes of mankind, for Christ is man himself, humiliated by man and rising to save him and bring him back to God, after having overwhelmed the forces which oppress him. Those forces express themselves in the life of mankind through the tyrants, who are anti-Christ, the opposite of Christ, the men in whose mouth words take the opposite meaning. As we see it in the " Prophétie sur les Nations " love becomes destruction. " Bread " brings with it pictures of famine and revolt, and it will be so until with " Joy " the real Christ comes, with his outstretched arms, symbol of reconciliation and bliss. " Liberté Guide Nos Pas " not only contains very moving poems prompted directly by events like " Fort Montluc " and " Otages " but also symbolical poems full of meaning and beauty like " La Colombe ", one of the most important of Emmanuel's symbols. " La Colombe ", the Holy Ghost, the message of God the Holy Spirit, which lies in wait in words pregnant with meaning, waiting for the poet for liberation, for the restoration of the sacred meaning. In the poem " La Colombe " the poet attempts to give a cosmic vision of man and to save with words life threatened with destruction. Emmanuel has been constantly preoccupied with the problem of language. " Hölderlin, ou le Poète Fou " is the failure of language. " Orphiques " shows the same concern with the power of words. There we have the strange journey of the poet who retires from a reality of frustration and returns to the beginning of life and language, when God created the woman from the primal androgyne. The essences which preceded the words are part of Eternity and God. If one could rediscover the very essence of the words, the words would produce a state of infinite mental potentiality which is one of the attributes of Eternity. As we shall see, the problem of language still preoccupies Emmanuel in " Sodome " and continues to do so in poems which have recently been published and form part of a forthcoming work " Babel ". " La Chanson du Dé à Coudre " (" The Song of the Thimble ") an everyday object which suggests the humble but constant preoccupations of the poet—God, Love and Life or rather Love, sinless love as the medium to reach God and the eternal life, is a collection which contains some of Emmanuel's finest and purest poetry. Though there are what one could describe

as pure poetic states, states of ecstasy, there is of course no pure
poetry, for poetry is made of words, and words are not pure
crystal perfectly transparent to the light of the soul in communion with Eternity, but grains of glass with a shape and
colour which can never be completely abolished so that
absolute purity always remains beyond human communication.   Musical notes, algebraical symbols, may produce certain results, if certain rules of mathematical reasoning or musical composition are followed, but language symbols stand for
images, ideas or emotions which vary for each individual,
and if the poet goes from the poetic ecstasy to the words,
the reader goes or attempts to go from the words to the poetic
ecstasy, but the words have a meaning and the ecstasy and he
pure poetry only lie in the state which precedes or follows the
poetry, but never in the poem itself.   Emmanuel is very much
aware of the limitations of words :

> Ce que rien n'a su dire
> Le néant seul le dit
> L'âme craint et désire
> Ce langage interdit
>
> Comme verre elle tremble
> Au souffle du verrier
> Qui la veut transparente
> A son éternité.

Poetry is something mysterious, some kind of undefinable
state in which eternity lives.   The human soul is the mirror
of its creator and the poet is the mouthpiece of undefinable
forces :

> Poètes
> Cailloux dans la bouche
> D'un demiurge bégayant
> Qui chante ? la roche
> Ou bien le vent ?
> Le coquillage
> Ou bien l'Océan ?

he only lives by his words,

> Moi, je suis la souche
> Sur pied pourrie
> Seuls ces vers qui bougent
> Me prêtent vie.

Whether he transmutes the harrowing situation through which he has lived, the emotions which he has experienced, or tries to find out his relationship with God and the Universe, Emmanuel can be extremely moving. Poems like " Arbres d'Artères ", " J'ai dans le sang l'odeur des pluies ", or most of those contained in the section " Dieu Parle " illustrate those points. " Arbres d'Artères " seems to me to deserve to be quoted in full :

> Arbre d'artères
> En moi planté
> Un oiseau-lierre
> T'a ligoté
>
> Dans la poitrine
> Siffle l'azur
> On assassine
> Même les murs
>
> Aigue, la balle
> Vrille le cœur
> Le ciel spirale
> et l'ombre meurt
>
> Soleil, hélice
> D'éternité
> D'une si lisse
> Vélocité
>
> Le sang qui gicle
> Dore l'été
> De ses magiques
> Rayons blessés.

Here we have thoughts and feelings expressed in a way in which words are given their full value of poetic ambiguity and creative power, here we have a sample of the cosmic imagination of the poet and of his acute consciousness of the power of words. It is also difficult not to quote from that accomplished poem " Rien non n'est ineffable " which expresses both the oneness of life dear to Blake and Keats and a rather Valéry-like attitude towards the power of silence, induced silence, pregnant with possibilities.

Most of the poems of " La Chanson du Dé à Coudre ". are very short, some of them have no more than three or four lines, and generally express one single mood. That means that there are no transitions ; the poetic emotion remains as pure as possible and when it is exhausted the poem is finished. The poems are the records of the fleeting thoughts and emotions which flashed through the mind and sensitiveness of the poet ; they are records full of freshness and genuineness ; they seem the unartful notations of a human consciousness, yet the sheer musical beauty of some of them is such as to make the reader feel that there could hardly be a happier and more perfect expression.

In " Sodome " Emmanuel attempts to write an epic of creation. The poem is divided into two parts : (1) Paradise lost, through the sin of sex ; it starts from the myth of Lot's wife turned into salt and silence and self-inflicted agony owing to the journey through past errors. (2) The birth of the song, which is a difficult blend of metaphysics and æsthetics. One cannot help thinking of Milton and one realizes once more the uniqueness of " Paradise Lost ". Of course the aims of the two poets are different, for while Milton accepts the Bible as it is, and applies to it his extraordinary genius, Emmanuel's poem is, above all, symbolical ; even when there is a narrative, as in the first part, it is extremely weak, and in the second part of the poem he tries to bring to life a new theory of language. Although Emmanuel has not completely succeeded in his aims, one cannot fail to be truly impressed by his achievement which shows that he has outstanding gifts. " Sodome " confirms the view that a long philosophical poem cannot be sustained without a narrative as a unifying thread. Milton found in

Satan " the objective correlative " and all his symbolism is
linked with it. Satan is the main *dramatis persona* of the first
six books and his presence casts its shadow over the whole
development of the other six books. Milton's characters,
human or supernatural, are on the whole prototypes showing the general characteristics of ordinary humanity. Their
actions and feelings are at times reminiscent of men's actions
and feelings. In Emmanuel there are no prototypes, there are
only metaphysical problems and concepts born from the Old
Testament and dealt with by a poet who has read Freud. The
Old Testament supplies the myths which in the end can be reduced to one only Christ-man, and Freud supplies the imagery
which is markedly sexual. Christ is the Adam of Paradise
Lost or Orpheus in the underworld, the eternal sufferer, the
eternally reborn, who will live supreme in God's unity
with the end of life. Christ is the Son of Man who will
be liberated by the end of man ; that anthropocentrism
explains the passage from the ethical to the æsthetic plane,
from the original sin to the word. This world, our world
could only be because of the wound which is the woman to
man, because of her very imperfection source of creation
and also of the death of Christ. This world is liberated by
the Word which is born from Christ's wound. The Word
is the feminine part of man, and the means for man to create
Space and Time and the movement which lasts until stony
silence freezes the earth.

 " Sodome " shows some very interesting aspects of Emmanuel's thought which is indeed in harmony with his time.
For him, beginning and end, which were once opposed,
meet in man's finite existence, and God, whose essence seems
to be to create man, merges with man when man is pure.

> Gloire à l'homme en qui se contemplent sans une ombre
> l'Origine et la Fin si longtemps ennemies
> dont l'étreinte incarnée en un vrai corps, colonne
> orante ! élève au front du Père un ciel humain,
> une Face où le temps transfigure ses larmes
> où dieu justifié se perd en l'homme pur.

Emmanuel's conception is that of the withdrawal of Milton,

> Mais Ton regard, se retirant au noir des âges
> et me livrant à l'air cruel, laissa ce corps
> séparé pour l'éternité de son Image
> peinte en néant sur la rétine de la Mort.

and also of Valéry, that creation is the flaw in the diamond of the universe, creation which God could not make perfect because it would have meant self-destruction.

> . . . Pitié ! mon repentir fut-il blasphème,
> j'ose me repentir d'être né de Tes doigts
> de sentir à mon flanc la blessure suprême
> qu'effrayé de me voir parfait Tu me portas.

That passage on creation is followed by a Narcissistic interpretation of the oneness of man, before the division or the knowledge of sex. This passage is reminiscent of Valéry but is more abstruse, more luxuriant, more emotional, more loaded with sexual symbolism than anything Valéry ever wrote ; it ends with the consummation of the original sin which here is obviously and unambiguously the sexual act. Then, in a beautiful passage which shows the range of Emmanuel's poetic imagination follows the vision of Adam fleeing God's anger, away from Eden which he will forever regret. Adam could have redeemed himself and his posterity, he could have softened his creator's wrath if instead of fleeing he had chosen Christ's humility and nakedness, and braved God's anger before the curse ; he would then have won God's mercy. But the first man took to flight ever pursued by the burning eye of consciousness fastened upon him, and dragging in his wake all the miseries which he bestowed upon his posterity.

> Eût-il, plus prompt que dieu
> dans le panique désarroi de la Colère
> avancé d'un seul pas vers l'Image, rompant
> la lumière enchantée qui givre l'œil humide

et retournant cet œil vers la toute douceur,
eût-il vêtu de Christ sa nudité dernière
avant que dieu l'ait pu maudire ! un seul regard
d'infini repentir alors l'eût accompli :

Abraham discovers what has been the failure of Adam ; he
recovers the unique vision and sees God whom he asks to
have pity on all those who are banished from His presence,
whose absence is their suffering, their hell. But not even
the very name of God could save those sufferers who pursue
through the sexual act a unity impossible to achieve. " Let
them realize," says Abraham, " who they are, let them know
that their wound is the voice of Christ who is the real man
eternally wounded, eternally redeemed, and then they will
hear his voice and will return to oneness." And from the
" wound of Christ" is born the word and the woman whose
birth sealed nothingness and made life.

S'ouvrent, à la hauteur du cœur, deux lèvres

This passage

Mais mon corps est toujours ailleurs en des postures
innombrables : son affreux râle de bonheur
je l'entends dans la chambre voisine
                                        O mensonge

d'un rêve trop lucide et qui ne peut saisir
le corps en même temps, au même lieu que l'âme !
Je cours je cours environné de mon odeur
mon sépulcre ambulant mon éternelle absence.

shows that Emmanuel shares in the ideas of his time, the
ideas of Sartre and of Valéry, the " creux toujours futur ",
the realization that man is always what he is not, and is
never what he is.

When one reads Emmanuel one cannot fail to think of
Dylan Thomas. Both poets draw most of their symbols
and myths from the Bible and their imagery from the reading
of Freud, and both have at times a tendency to pure verbalism
which is obviously the result of their Surrealist way of writing.

The difference is that Dylan Thomas is more Freudian than Emmanuel who remains obsessed by his sense of sin.   Dylan Thomas also retains towards sin an attitude which is a combination of Freud and the Old Testament.   Sex is creative and destructive, and the poem "Paradise Regained"

> I by the tree of thieves all glory's sawbones
> unsex the skeleton this mountain's minute.

shows that the problem for Thomas still consists in reconciling those two aspects of sex.   His later poetry shows that his attitude to sex has become more and more Freudian.   For Emmanuel the main urge of sex associated with sin is self-annihilation ; but his poetry like that of Thomas is packed with at times an extraordinarily powerful sexual imagery.

> Le grand ciel écartant de l'aile tes genoux
> s'incline sur tes seins en frissonnant, et plonge
> son plumage sacré dans le sillon du songe.
> Il s'ébroue, et la chair profonde à son désir
> est une eau douce au cygne ardent qui prend le large,
> cependant qu'étendue dans les âges, tu sens
> soudain s'abandonner, l'aile morte et froissée
> le Cygne (ou l'Ange) entre tes jambes resserrées,
> à la brusque et nerveuse étreinte que l'aigu
> d'un cri—d'or et brûlant jusqu'aux larmes—relâche.

And to give an idea of Emmanuel's achievements and capability of controlling words through a musical unit, which is not the line but a complete paragraph, one might quote the merry Hosannah of man to God.

> Je chante un feu parfait sur ma légère cendre,
> un parfait abandon de plaines à Tes pieds
> Seigneur : la saison sobre où les eaux se recueillent
> à peine loin m'effleure-t-elle que je meurs
>
> Heureux d'être étendu selon Ta Face, ô Père
> du voyageur ! s'il m'est laissé cet arbre seul
> ce peuplier qui m'attendait depuis l'enfance,
> pour gage que je surgirai d'entre les morts.

Un arbre, une fontaine : ô plaie vive ! j'écoute
mort, d'un autre que moi sourdre à jamais le sang
et le murmure emplit mon épaisseur de terre.

Il me garde poreux et souple dans la Mort.
Un jour, après des siècles d'astres, le silence
reviendra sur mes lèvres nues, et le printemps.

On the whole, " Sodome ", which contains passages of
striking beauty, is too heterogeneous, and lacks the unifying
force of a central character or theme ; we pass from the
fundamentally religious and moral plane to a combination
of metaphysics and æsthetics. In spite of the splendid
visionary powers of the poet which operate on a cosmic
scale, the images are too often not images apprehensible to
the senses but purely conceptual images or arrangements of
words which doubtless contain the abstract belief of the poet
but do not evoke any sensuous response in the reader.   But
this type of poetry, in which very few poets have succeeded,
shows, like the rest of Emmanuel's poetry, flashes of genius
which might yet make of him one of the most important
French poets of the years to come.

We might conclude this brief study of Emmanuel's poetry
by saying a few words about a poem which is amongst his
most recent publications and which shows him at his best.   It
is " Grotte, Femme ou Cité " probably from " Babel ", an
unpublished work.   It is a remarkable poem which presents
a cosmic vision of man, a vision of timelessness and oneness
of man past and future, of human life and nature.   It is a
poem which contains elements of great poetry, and which
shows Pierre Emmanuel at his best, not only as a poet of
apocalyptic vision but as a maker of striking images and
majestic music which can conjure up in a background of
metaphysical *Angst* the vision of man, the problems of his
destiny and the complexity of feelings which they produce.
The imagery and symbols of the poem are biblical and sexual.
The sexual act, the source of pleasure and the goal of man, is
also supreme consciousness, the revelation of Adam, and is

I

the image of Death towards which man tends.   It corresponds
to one of the most fundamental desires of man, the desire to
return to nothingness.   That poem contains some remarkable
passages such as the following :

> Cet homme grelottant d'avoir quitté son toit
> sa rue, le quartier fade où ses péchés végètent
> ses vieux remords grattant leurs escarres, ses dieux
> tissant leur toile au fond des temples et des bouges
> l'odeur enfin ! arquant les jambes sous le poids
> d'un monde au roulis lourd qui tend la robe rouge
> saint environnement, chaleur du ventre, peur !
> cet homme ne connaît de paix qu'au sein des filles
> plus que la mer indifférentes et roulant
> selon la lune sous les corps qu'elles naufragent
> l'un sur l'autre, d'un tour machinal de leurs reins.

It has been remarked that the poem " Sodome " evokes the
name of Milton who had already illuminated the road which
Emmanuel tries to follow.   Emmanuel's relative youth and
remarkable gifts are such that he might yet justify this association with the author of " Paradise Lost "

V

SURREALISM

THE history of Surrealism is too well-known to leave room for a new presentation of its main developments. To quote only two books, " l'Histoire du Surréalisme " by Maurice Nadeau and " L'Anthologie de l'Humour Noir " by André Breton, cover that ground pretty thoroughly.

Surrealism as an organized literary movement, conscious of itself and endowed with a body of doctrinal principles, is relatively new. It dates from René Gill who analysed it and explained it at length in a criticism of Rimbaud's " Les Illuminations ". This was what one might call the first thoroughly Surrealist poem ; together with it we had the unique influence of Lautréamont and, after him, Jarry, Apollinaire and the famous manifestos of André Breton, who has been the most vigorous exponent of the Surrealist doctrine. On the other hand, the philosophical beliefs which underlie Surrealism are extremely old ; they find their first expression in a philosophy which was probably co-ordinated by the philosopher Zoroaster, who lived in the ninth century B.C. That philosophy pervaded the Syrian and the Jewish world and in the sixth century B.C. spread to the Hindu world. Later on its main principles reappear in the Cabala, an occult philosophy made up of some Hebrew traditional interpretations of the Old Testament. The cardinal principle of that philosophy, strongly akin to the philosophy of Plato and his world of ideas and essences, is that God is the centre and that each individual soul of man or nature is part of it and can only find completion in it. The world is the thought of God expressed, unfolded, and waiting to be read by the great mind who will be endowed with the power to do so ; but this world of realities perceived by the senses, is only a reflection of the world which lies beyond the senses, a world apprehensible only through the word. Everything in this world in which we live is symbolical. Life is symbolical of an immortal life, art is symbolical of life and tends to reveal the immortal life. All true poetry is bound to be symbolical. In order to enter into full relationship with His creation, God took upon Himself human shape and came to the world, in the person of Christ, the Word ever present in the world of man or in the heart of those who will it. Man could not understand God's word and had to transpose it in order that it could become part of him, and yet the word is used with the force and meaning which it had when man heard it from God, and it remains the symbol which can link up man with God, and the means of discovering the reality which lies beyond. Poetry becomes thus a language, or if one wishes, a collection of cabalistic signs which can conjure up a vision of eternity. The real poet is the one who can have that vision, who has the power of seeing beyond Time and of merging as Blake said into " One Man ". As it is well known these principles were constantly alive in men's minds, and consciously or subconsciously are the foundation of great thought and great poetry. They can be found in Plato, in Plotinus, in the Zohar, and in the philosophy of Jacob Boehme who was Blake's main source of inspiration ; we find them in Swedenborg who certainly influenced Baudelaire and Rimbaud ; we find them at the source of Schopenhauer's world of ideas, and if we bear in mind the subjectivism of Hume, we come to realize that Symbolism and Surrealism could not fail to prevail in litera-ture after " Les Fleurs du Mal ". Indeed, it was Baudelaire who first laid great stress on the value of dreams. It was he who said " it is through dreams that man communicates with the dark dream by which he is surrounded," and it was Baudelaire who set the example of using any kind of artificial means to reach that oniric state, but Baudelaire, obsessed as he was by the idea of sin, remained ever aware that

drug-taking was an immoral act, an act which infringed upon
the laws of God ; he also realized that drugs could, in the
end, reveal only what was there, that is to say the man that he
was. It was Rimbaud who, with a kind of saint-like passion
and with the absolute self-abnegation of a mystic, was convinced that he might perhaps be the great expected poet who
would be able to unfold before man's eyes the very meaning
of creation ; he was therefore prepared to undergo any
experience, even if it were to lead him to madness or death.
" The poet," said Rimbaud, " makes himself a seer by means
of a long, vast and reasoned derangement of all the senses—
all forms of love, suffering or madness ; he searches within
himself and consumes all the poisons to be found there pre-
serving all the quintessence." There lies the source of his
Satan-like pride which led him to equate himself with God
and which, once he had lived Hell on earth as he explained
in " Une Saison en Enfer ", led him to the renunciation of
poetry. For Rimbaud, great poetry was Greek poetry,
Dionysiac poetry ; the poet was for him the seer whose
vision penetrates beyond the veil of appearances, and has the
power to hear the voice of the eternal. Here it is interesting
to contrast the transcendentalism of Rimbaud with that of
Valéry for instance. For Valéry poetry was language.
Language created poetry. For Rimbaud language if properly
handled in poetry, could reveal the hidden mysteries of the
world in whose existence he believed, and for a time he
thought that he had discovered that new way of using
language. Ideas in the Platonic sense were going to become
the ultimate aim of all arts and it is remarkable to note that
both in novelists like Balzac and philosophers like Schopenhauer, we find in the second half of the nineteenth century a
strong and widespread belief in the existence of an ideal world
beyond reality. That principle was the foundation of Symbolism and of Surrealism. Rimbaud appeared at a time
when the French artistic scene was under the strong influence
of the Parnassians and when Baudelaire had opened new
fields to the poetry of suggestion. Rimbaud increased the

suggestive power of poetry, and without him the Surrealist movement would probably not have come to life. It was Rimbaud who initiated in France the literature of the sub-conscious ; Baudelaire had tried before him to plumb the depths of his " ennui " and " spleen " but it was Rimbaud who systematically sought to establish communication with the inner-self which is the self of all. The Surrealist theory flows directly from Rimbaud's æsthetic doctrine. " Sur-realism is based on belief in the superiority of certain forms of association which have been too neglected, in the omnipo-tence of dreams, and in the free and disinterested play of thought," said A. Breton, in " Premier Manifeste du Sur-réalisme ". The poet, according to Rimbaud, is the voice of the eternal, he is beyond good and evil, and the poet's duty is to penetrate beyond realities and to try to express the ideas which the universal memory, or *anima mundi*, throws up at each stage of the life of man. Rimbaud sought beyond belief or disbelief ecstatic union with God, and strangely enough had a great influence on Catholic writers. At the beginning of his life and during his creative period he tried with his abnormal pride to be the equal of God but he came to realize that he belonged, as he said, to " the inferior race ", that he needed Christ, and he died a Catholic. His journey was an arduous one but it bore fruit. But however great Rimbaud's achievements were, they are far from being the only source of inspiration of the Surrealist movement. One must not forget Lautréamont who like Rimbaud sacrificed himself to his art ; one must not forget Victor Hugo whose visionary power not only influenced Rimbaud himself, but remains unsurpassed by any of the poets who have found inspiration in his work. Then there is Guillaume Apollinaire who had already died before " Littérature ", the first Surrealist review, had begun to appear. Apollinaire, like all true poets, believed that poetry alone could reveal the mysteries of existence. He sought to explore, through his poetry, fields yet untouched which were later to become the favourite grounds of the Surrealists. " La Jolie Rousse " an extremely

moving and very effective poem which he wrote before 1918
contains, in its lyrical, autobiographical, and didactic strains,
the whole journey of the poet, and his poetic beliefs.

Soyez indulgents quand vous nous comparez
A ceux qui furent la perfection de l'ordre
Nous qui quêtons partout l'aventure.

. . . .

Nous voulons nous donner de vastes et d'étranges domaines
Où le mystère en fleurs s'offre à qui veut le cueillir
Il y a là des feux nouveaux des couleurs jamais vues
Mille phantasmes impondérables
Auxquels il faut donner de la réalité

. . . .

Pitié pour nous qui combattons toujours aux frontières
De l'illimité et de l'avenir
Pitié pour nos erreurs pitié pour nos péchés.

A poem which has a greater range than " La Jolie Rousse ",
and which shows the same qualities in an even higher degree,
is " Les Collines " and there we read :

Où donc est tombée ma jeunesse
Tu vois que flambe l'avenir
Sache que je parle aujourd'hui
Pour annoncer au monde entier
Qu'enfin est né l'art de prédire.

" Le Chant de l'Amour " brings together the connotations
and images suggested by the word love, and " Les Soupirs
du Servant de Dakar " describes with great pathos the harrowing thoughts of a negro torn from his native soil and plunged
in the turmoil of modern war. There is no doubt that
" Calligrammes " and " Alcools " are the works of a remarkable poet whose influence is foremost in Surrealist literature.

Any brief survey of the world of literature shows that the
fundamental principles which the Surrealists have annexed
for their school, have been the foundation of most achievements in creative art. The Surrealists assert the importance
of Freud in the exploration of that source of art, the subconscious ; Sophocles and Shakespeare did not know as well

as Freud, the orderly, numbered roads of the subconscious, but great creators that they were, they were aware of the existence of all the problems which Freud systematically unfolded later on, and they brought them out in a form apprehensible to the senses, which became part of that human consciousness which Freud described. The belief, mentioned by André Breton in the second manifesto of Surrealism, that " there exists in the life of the mind a point when life and death, the real and the imaginary, past and future, the communicable and uncommunicable, the high and the low cease to be perceived as contrary ", is on the whole, the very foundation of poetic inspiration whose description from the myth of Orpheus to Supervielle recurs constantly through literature. This is what Supervielle says :

I myself need this clarity all the more because I am obscure by nature and have a longing for lucidity. In my case there is no poetry that does not bring in a certain confusion. I try to set out in it guiding lights, to resolve this confusion for the sake of a certain degree of order without destroying the mystery, that element of darkness necessary, as Gide has shown, in every work of art ; my efforts consist in making the conscious collaborate with the unconscious, in making one straight line out of one or more broken lines.

In my case the logic of the story teller keeps a very sharp eye on the wandering fancy of the poet and keeps it in step. Some people have said that I was a Surrealist. Far from it. I hold very strongly that the guiding thread of a poem should be obvious, and that does not interest the Surrealists, at least in so far as they are Surrealists. . . .

Bergson speaking about instinct says that it is surrounded by a fringe of intelligence. So I prefer the mystery of poetry to be ringed round with intelligence. If I draw a veil, it is instinctively, and it is my hope that what is there is only the veil of poetry and not that of obscurity.

The only difference between the Surrealists and Supervielle or any poet of importance who knows the meaning of what is called inspiration is, that the pure Surrealists in their " dogmatic belief in the supreme value of the irrational ", have

ended in verbalism or silence. Such is the case of Tristan
Tzara, Soupault, and many others. The poets who like
Eluard and Aragon succeeded in making full use of Surrealism by dominating it, by writing according to their
personalities and not according to dogmas, show the same
respect as Supervielle for " le fil conducteur " in the poem
and recognize the importance of the collaboration of consciousness and subconsciousness as the foundation of great
art. Attempts have been made by some of the Surrealists
to turn Bergson into an apostle of the Irrational, but Bergson
merely insisted on the value of those realms or rather those
outer fringes which consciousness could not explore. He
insisted indeed on the value of subjectivity, but it was Laforgue
and not Bergson who cried " A bas la raison ". From
pagan mythology to the Christian myth, the Gods or God
never spoke to the human being directly but always through
a being who shared in the essences of both and joined them.
Apollo spoke through Orpheus who could use human words,
and Christ is the very word of God. The absolute transcendent mystical experience, timeless and undivided, can only be
communicated at the price of a compromise, through the
word which can be the magic sign revelatory of another
world, but which remains at the same time the very foundation of reason.

The claims of the Surrealists were exaggerated. Their
achievements are limited but their importance as a revolutionary movement which fought for liberty and progress in
art is undeniable. Born from the disillusionment of war,
war which never fails to shake to its foundations the human
consciousness and to question the value of most principles
of organized life, Surrealism set itself as a progressive *avant-
garde* movement towards a new age, an age in which the
individual would be freed from the bonds or the chains of
family, religion, society as we know them, and would live
as only ideal beings could live. That age is still far off, but
Surrealism certainly succeeded in giving the artist a greater
awareness of the problems of his time and in renewing some

of the sources of artistic creation.   Nowadays Surrealism in
its doctrinal form is not dead but it is certainly not lively and
resplendent.   Most of the articles of faith of that so-called
new doctrine have returned to where they belonged, to
poetry ; and we discover them in the works of all important
poets, including of course the one who is supposed to be the
most intellectual, Valéry. For Valéry could extract more
from the fascinating explorations of his consciousness which
are terribly similar to states of induced dreams, in the course
of which the mind watches and lives through strange con-
fusions, than Tristan Tzara from the mist of his subconscious.

If there is one realm in which the Œdipus complex is
strong, it is in the realm of literature.   There each generation
of writers seeks to destroy the generation which brought it
life.   The Romantics sought to destroy the Classics, the
Surrealists sought to destroy the middle class which had
fathered them and nurtured them.   Their dream could probably be summed up in the words of Gide : " Table rase.
J'ai tout balayé.   C'en est fait !   Je me dresse sur la terre
vierge derrière le ciel à repeupler." Consciousness and
rationalism were the cardinal virtues of the middle class ;
the Surrealists sought to abolish them and to replace them
by the pre-eminence of the subconscious, in a world which
remained unavoidably objective.   The Surrealists in their
negativist attitude would have liked to destroy that objective
world but it could not be done, for though existence might
change its forms, its essence remains unchangeable and makes
complete destruction an impossibility.   So the Surrealists
sought to destroy language by breaking it up, and by showing
its inadequacy to render any deep experience of the psyche.
But their attempt was condemned to failure.   Intellectuals
could not destroy intellect, for one cannot be intellectually
violent except by refusing to be intellectual and replacing
logic by shouts and screams ; in their desire to destroy their
fathers the Surrealists allied themselves with the Communists
who share in their negativist attitude, but for the Communist,
negation and violence are only a means to the end of political

power, while the Surrealist remained condemned by definition to aimless impulses of violence for violence's sake. The working class which they seek to defend cannot in any way apprehend and appreciate their destructive creations which only appeal to the few experts, to the intellectuals and to those in search of curious sensations.

The only important poets of the Surrealist movement are Aragon and Eluard. If we examine both of them in the context of Surrealism we realize that both owe their poetic achievements to the fact that their strong poetic personalities transcended Surrealism and only took from it the elements which they could fuse into a poetry which was not the embodiment of a doctrine, but the expression of their selves. Aragon's break with Surrealism is far more pronounced than Eluard's, and in fact his best poetry, the love and war poetry, owes nothing to Surrealism and is a return to old French traditions. Aragon leapt into fame with " Le Crève-cœur " and " Les Yeux d'Elsa ". Those two volumes contain his best poetry and poems like " Les Lilas et les Roses ", " La Nuit de Dunkerque ", " La Nuit d'Exil ", " Richard II Quarante ", have great tenseness and poignancy of feeling. These qualities are conveyed by the moving music of lines packed with images of great literary effectiveness. They conjure up the aura of France's history and all the mysterious and powerful sentiments associated with the lost dear being which was France. They are not free from the usual defects of Aragon's poetry—rhetoric, extreme technical facility, mere punning and jingle of words—and yet, on the whole, they are of their kind, very often accomplished poetry which will have a place in French literature, in the tradition of genuine lyricism which reaches from Villon to Verlaine. France's misfortunes and miseries stirred the very roots of the whole past of France, dormant in the poet, and telescoping the extremes, the France of 1940 becomes the France of the Middle Ages, the France of those legends and mythical heroes like Lancelot and Tristan in whose lives the ideals of love and honour were the guiding lights.

Je veille, il se fait tard, la nuit du Moyen-Age couvre d'un manteau
noir cet univers brisé,

says Aragon. He discovered in his love for his country the
sources of lyrical and epic poetry, poetry which is undoubtedly successful in its kind. Aragon's name can conjure
up not only the names of Villon and Verlaine but also, by
his brilliance and virtuosity, those of Rostand and Banville.
But too often virtuosity inebriates him, and his poetry ends
at times in mere verbalism void of poetic substance. Eluard
seems to me a more important poet. His achievements are
greater than those of Aragon ; besides Aragon's reputation
in the English-speaking world and even in France is well
established, probably too well established for its foundations ;
moreover, he gives the impression that he has said what he
has to say, while Eluard still remains unpredictable. It therefore seems to me more interesting to try to assess the importance of Surrealism in the best and most accomplished of its
living representatives.

VI

PAUL ELUARD

One must have chaos
To give birth to a dancing star
                                        Nietzsche

ONE of the main beliefs of the Surrealists was that poetry
was everywhere, belonged to everyone, and should not
be the product of the work of one isolated individual but the
result of the work of all.   The Surrealist poets put their creed
into practice, and they were one of the few, perhaps the
only *cénacle* of artists which has been based on real friendship.
The words of Blake, " the life of the imagination is the real
life ", could have been their motto ; everything that can
be imagined exists and imagination is the way to reach the
" great One " source of life, and painters and poets applied
all the resources of their art, and their power of vision towards
the liberation of the subconscious.   Eluard's poetry contains
many names of painters who were and still are his friends,
among them Max Ernst, Picasso, Chirico and Salvador Dali,
all of them talented painters endowed with freshness of mind
whose explorations and creations are amongst the supreme
achievements of our times.   Picasso is for Eluard *l'ami sublime*.   René Clair and André Breton worked with Eluard
to produce the book " Ralentir travaux ", and André Breton
is with Eluard the author of an uncommon and interesting
book from the theoretical point of view, called " L'Immaculée
Conception ".   Eluard and Aragon submitted themselves to
gruelling experiences in order to prove that the poetic mind
can explore all the aspects of the life of the psyche, from
madness to sanity, and retain its equilibrium.   This proved

to them that what seems to be the most genuine state of
delirium can be induced, and can take place while reason
notes its intricate and complex development. Reason can
follow and describe the irrational, as this experiment demon-
strated, but it must be said that Eluard is perhaps the only
one of the Surrealist poets who succeeded completely in this
tour de force and Aragon, who is, after Eluard, the most
important Surrealist poet, wrote his really valuable and
significant poetry when genuine lyricism was the source
of his inspiration. But Eluard, even in his earliest poetry,
which is at times so Surrealist that it can only be apprehended
as scintillations from the night of the poems and not as
a complete living experience, is on the whole successful.
His earliest poetry shows already the marks of outstanding
talent.

Consider for instance the little poem " Vache ". This
poem is full of fantasy. It comes perilously close to a play
on words, yet it escapes that pitfall and remains like the
graceful caprice of some nymph or impish gnome of the
woods. The same could be said about " Poisson " or about
most of the poems of " Les Animaux et leurs Hommes "
which show the same whimsicality, humour and skilful
juggling with words verging on the pun and yet avoiding it.

The volumes which followed—" Capitale de la Douleur ",
" La Pyramide Humaine ", " L'Amour la Poésie ", and
" A Toute Epreuve "—contain good poetry, although at that
time Eluard was writing under strong Surrealist influences.
Sometimes one prefers his prose ; a rich prose packed with
images, carefully integrated, but shot through every now
and then with a kind of poetry in which there is a theme.
" Amoureuses " is an example of this.

> Elles ont les épaules hautes
> Et l'air malin
> Ou bien des mines qui déroutent
> La confiance est dans la poitrine
> A la hauteur où l'aube de leurs seins se lève
> Pour dévêtir la nuit.

"La Rose Publique" marks the apex of Eluard's Sur-realist tendencies and can be regarded as a turning-point in his poetry. The poet himself says : " L'objectivité poétique n'existe que dans la succession, dans l'enchaînement de tous les éléments subjectifs dont le poète est jusqu'à nouvel ordre, non le maître mais l'esclave." The poems in this volume are also autobiographical ; most of the incidents described, most of the images, have a relation to the poet's life. The poem "Comme deux gouttes d'eau" is Eluard's confession. It suggests the subterranean ramifications of his life, his attempts to detach himself from everyday life or from his surround-ings, his dreams of other lands and other worlds, and what remains of it all :

> De tout ce que j'ai dit de moi que reste-t-il
> J'ai conservé de faux trésors dans des armoires vides
> Un navire inutile joint mon enfance à mon ennui.

—the boat for his journey across the Pacific, his dreams, his visions symbolized, as so often, by the woman and embodied in a moving and extraordinarily intense poetry :

> Filles de rien prêtes à tout
> Sœurs des fleurs sans racines
> Sœurs des enfants rebelles
> Minuscules
> Indifférentes
> Réduites à l'intelligence
> A la raison à en mourir
> Réduite dans vos secrets
> Etrangères délaissées
> Mes lointaines compagnes
> Aux chairs sentimentales
> Belles à peine belles mais toujours belles
> Plus simples que le malheur
> Plus précieuses que la beauté
> De vos lèvres abattues
> De votre sourire éffondré
> Vous me confiez vos poisons
> O mithridatisées.

and the poem contains a record of distant moments of the
poet's life or of incidents which he has seen.

> J'ai vu mon meilleur ami
> Creuser dans les rues de la ville
> Dans toutes les rues de la ville un soir
> Le long tunnel de son chagrin.
> Il offrait à
> To tes les femmes
> Une rose privilégiée
> Une rose de rosée
> Pareille à l'ivresse d'avoir soif.

That incident is apparently true ; André Breton is said to
have presented once to a woman a rose which he described
as a forget-me-not.

The poem is certainly written in a Surrealist mood, but
it seems that the imagination of the poet has followed a
kind of given course across the dark sky of the page and so
we have, not a random race of exploding stars, but the illumin-
ating blaze of a comet's tail which we can follow in the joy of
our undisappointed expectations.   The passages beginning :

> J'ai vu le soleil quitter la terre
> . . . .
> J'ai vu le sablier du ciel et de la mer se renverser
> . . . .
> Et j'ai vu naître l'imperceptible
> la nuit rêvée.

are packed with beautiful and effective images congruent to
the theme of the poem.   The passage for instance :

> J'ai vu une femme regarder son enfant nouveau-né
> Comme une tuile enlevée d'un toit
> Son enfant en progrès sur l'homme

contains a powerful image which vividly conveys the mother's
thoughts piercing right through the existence of her newly
born child in the same way as gnomes or fairies sometimes
lift a tile from the roof of a house in order to discover what

takes place beneath. That simile is compressed but it holds together and is all the more effective because it is pruned and reduced to its bare essentials. "La Rose Publique" contains remarkable poems which though they are difficult to grasp in their entirety are very effective. "Ce que dit l'Homme de Peine", for instance, has no central thread but a theme explored in an impressionistic way. From the very start the theme is given : "Un hiver tout en branches et nu comme un cadavre" ; and after a development "Il y a des démolitions plus tristes qu'un sou." The end echoes the beginning in a mood of rather sombre despair which overcomes the poet who walks down "plus bas parmi les routes abolies", and finds again

> Ce rêve déchiré désemparé tordu ridicule
> Cette harmonie en friche
> Cette peuplade qui mendie
>
> Parce qu'elle n'a voulu que de l'or
> Toute sa vie intacte
> Et la perfection de l'amour.

Another poem of that same collection has a title which is strangely reminiscent of the beginning of Kubla Khan :

> Elle se fit élever un palais qui ressemblait à un étang dans une forêt, car toutes les apparences réglées de la lumière étaient enfouies dans des miroirs, et le trésor diaphane de sa vertu reposait au fin fond des ors et des émeraudes, comme un scarabée.

Like Kubla Khan it has its source in a dream which the poet had had a few years before and which reappeared later as poetic material and with associations and connotations impossible to trace. The poem maintains throughout its dream-like atmosphere and ends with a passage which shows all the resources of Eluard's music and imagery :

> Cherchez la nuit
> Il fait beau comme dans un lit
> Ardente la plus belle des filles adorantes

. . . .

K

La plus belle des amantes
Offre ses mains tendues
Par lesquelles elle vient de loin
Du bout du monde de ses rêves
Par des escaliers de frissons et de lune au galop.

" La Rose Publique " is a landmark in the poetry of Eluard.
After having surveyed his past life, he takes his bearings and
sets off with the mind of a poet who knows what he wants
and who has a guiding star. To be true, that guiding star
existed before ; it shines in poems such as " L'Amour la
Poésie ", " Capitale de la Douleur " and others, but he had
neither reached the plenitude of his poetic power, nor the
full maturity of his personality. Already, before " La Rose
Publique ", love was the most important of Eluard's poetic
themes but his love, though all-embracing, was somehow
uncertain ; it could not abolish the future and his poetry, still
in its early developments profoundly surrealist, made use of
dreams and hallucinations and exploited to the point of
abstruseness the advantages of discontinuity and surprise. It
was at times like a mysterious world strewn with beautiful
images, colours and sounds, but difficult to penetrate.

With " Facile " and " Les Yeux Fertiles " a new chapter
begins. Eluard still retains his convictions about the value
of the subconscious as a source of great poetry ; but as his
life has now a steady centre round which everything revolves,
so his poetry will show more and more traces of that harmony
which is due to the application of the laws of numbers ; the
poetic experience, being really the very essence of the poet's
life, reflects the same obedience to the laws of harmony. The
past is now abolished, faded away in the night, the future is
completely veiled by the present and exists only in the present.
Nothing exists except the moment lived, ever renewed, and
Eluard walks on earth with love renewing every second of
his life. The whole being, spiritual and physical, is fused into
the moment lived, the moment which continuously solders
past and future into a whole. From these poems onwards,
Eluard's poetry begins to show a great concentration and purity.

Tu sacrifies le temps
A l'éternelle jeunesse de la flamme exacte
Qui voile la nature en la reproduisant

Femme tu mets au monde un corps toujours pareil
Le tien

and in " L'Entente " :

Belle à désirs renouvelés tout est nouveau
tout est futur.

" Les Yeux Fertiles " bears the mark of Eluard's ever-growing concern with some of the problems of daily life. Those were the years when the first rumblings, which were going to shake the world from 1940 to 1945, were heard in Spain and in China. Eluard, like many artists and intellectuals of his time, was deeply perturbed by the signs of the coming storm, and it was at this time that he wrote " the moment has come when all the poets have the right and the duty to maintain that they are closely merged into the daily life of other men ". The poet, more aware than the average human being of the subterranean stirrings of mankind, must be the " consciousness " of his fellow-beings, the beacon which rallies them and points to them the way. Eluard's poetry echoes more and more intensely the general pre-occupations of mankind. They sound a clarion call, " La Tête contre le Mur " for instance,

Prenez-y garde nous avons
Malgré la nuit qu'il couve
Plus de force que le ventre
De vos sœurs et de vos femmes
Et nous nous reproduirons
Sans elles mais à coups de hache
Dans vos prisons.

or the moving poem of " Le Front Couvert " which flows with the sap of human blood, and shows the poet torn and tormented by the violence of the problems of his time.

Ici j'ai ma part de ténèbres
Chambre secrète sans serrure sans espoir
Je remonte le temps jusqu'aux pires absences
Combien de nuits soudain
Sans confiance sans un beau jour sans horizon
Quelle gerbe rognée
Un grand froid de corail
Ombre du cœur
Ternit mes yeux qui s'entr'ouvent
Sans donner prise au matin fraternel.

There are poems like " Intimes " as graceful and ethereal as
a fairy dance.   This is a pæan to Love in which Eluard makes
full use of alliterations and repetitions and then ends with a
hexameter whose rhythm and evocative power are worthy
of Racine.

Et des jours et des nuits réglés par tes paupières.

On the whole, this volume of poems states the theme, which
together with the theme of love, forms the foundation of
Eluard's poetry—the conception of the poet or the artist as
the very consciousness of life.   Eluard has written poetry
which reaches beyond time towards the eternity which it
makes ; but he has also written poetry, and some of it most
important poetry, which is not only in time but where the
purity of the poet's heart reflects the age in which he lives.
The poem to " Pablo Picasso " tells us something about the
great painter " whose hands can shape space " and " who
can give life to worlds which lie buried under the eyelids ".
This poem also ends with two beautiful lines, two classical
hexameters whose meaning defies analysis.   The poet has
been talking about those dark daughters whom Picasso
painted and it is about them that he says :

Montrez-moi ces secrets qui unissent leurs tempes
A ces palais absents qui font monter la terre.

The other volumes " Cours Naturel ", " Donner à Voir ",
" Chanson Complète " which followed " Les Yeux Fertiles "

emphasize that preoccupation of Eluard with the problems of his time and with the sufferings of his fellow beings. In " Sans Age "—" Cours Naturel ", the poet says :

> Le ciel s'élargira
> Nous en avions assez
> D'habiter dans les ruines du sommeil.
>
> Nous aborderons tous une mémoire nouvelle
> Nous parlerons ensemble un langage sensible.

and then the very moving passage :

> O mes frères perdus
> Moi je vais vers la vie j'ai l'apparence d'homme
> Pour prouver que le monde est fait à ma mesure.

This passage reminds one of Supervielle for it shows the same sense of communion between man and nature, and sets man as the measure and the image of the cosmos ; but it has something more which we do not find in Supervielle's poetry which mostly deals with man in a state of innocence. It shows a strong sense of justice towards those who suffer ; indeed, the poet not only sympathizes with suffering, but seeks to put an end to it. " La vraie poésie est la négation de l'iniquité," said Baudelaire, and Eluard entitles one of his poems " Chanson Complète, Nulle Rupture ; la lumière et la conscience m'accablent d'autant de mystères, de misères que la nuit et les rêves", and in " Novembre 1936 ", a poem which certainly shows the strain of actuality he says

> Regardez travailler les bâtisseurs de ruines
> Ils sont riches patients ordonnés noirs et bêtes.

and concludes with the hope :

> Que l'homme délivré de son passé absurde
> Dresse devant son frère un visage semblable
> Et donne à la raison des ailes vagabondes.

For Eluard the poet is the seer who can look into the

future. He has a strong sense of duty and finds himself opposed to those who believe in art for art's sake or the refuge in the ivory tower. He believes that his duty is to warn men and to inspire them to struggle along the road which leads to greater happiness. The past, "Paradise Lost", the misty millennium of the Golden Age, holds no appeal for Eluard. What counts for him is the present and the future towards which he constantly reaches in order to transform it into a happy present. Eluard does not linger by the groves of the past. To live for him is to live in the present :

> Ton corps chante son assurance
> Tout vouloir tout pouvoir à jamais
> Ton espoir calme était un trésor fabuleux.

In the present we make the future ; to will is to make, with faith in the body which exists in the moment, and instead of going backward towards the past one must look forward

> Ne pas aller au cœur des autres : en sortir

in order to have :

> Mais la gloire de lire un bonheur sans limites
> Dans la simplicité des lignes du présent.

Side by side with poems which show his social preoccupations,

> Mais nos désirs sont moins lancinants dans la nuit
> Frères que cette étoile rouge
> Qui gagne malgré tout du terrain sur l'horreur.

Eluard continued to write poems in the Surrealist tradition which show a remarkable feeling for all the subtleties of music and a very fertile imagination. Although they lack organic unity they are held together by a unity of tone. The poem " Quelques-uns des mots qui jusqu'ici m'étaient mystérieusement interdits ", or " Où en étais-je ", come under

this heading.   The combination of Surrealism and conscious
effort produces a poem like " A l'Ombre de ma Porte " which
is a remarkable achievement.

" Vivre ", which begins the volume " Le Livre Ouvert ",
succeeds in conveying an intense experience, an experience
which in itself suggests a conception of life—and this conception is now transmuted into poetic terms.   Life for Eluard
is continuous, integral, and cosmic :

> Je me construis entier à travers tous les êtres
> A travers tous les temps au sol et dans les nues
> Saisons passantes je suis jeune
> Et fort à force d'avoir vécu
> Je suis jeune et mon sang s'élève sur mes ruines.

The individual separated from his background does not exist.
He exists only as a part of the whole in relation to the beings
and things which surround him, and although his consciousness seeks to define itself by finding out the line of demarcation
which separates it from the ambient world, consciousness is
ever invaded by its surroundings and exists in relation to
them.

> Mon âge m'accordait toujours
> De nouvelles raisons de vivre par autrui
> Et d'avoir en mon cœur le sang d'un autre cœur.

Life is love, the rest is nothingness :

> La grande règle
> Ce qui est digne d'être aimé
> Contre ce qui s'anéantit.

> Habitante d'un monde où sans toi je n'ai rien
> Ton cœur qui déjà dort oublie tout sauf mon cœur
> Dehors nos souvenirs nuits à flanc de journées
> Agitent nos liens sans pouvoir les briser.
> > "Je veux qu'elle soit R ine !"

One is strongly impressed by the fact that life for Eluard takes
place only in the present, and is a continuous emergence from

nothingness which surrounds it, literally eats up the moment lived and gapes at the vacuum ahead on the road which the self must tread. Life is thus always in the making but, in contrast with Valéry's absolute scepticism, Eluard believes in perfectibility. He believes in the value of human exertions to reach the good, and above all he believes in the value of the poet's exertions to bring to an end the iniquities and injustices of life. That attitude of Eluard, his conviction that the poet belongs first and foremost to his time and must try to influence it for the good, are quite in keeping with the Surrealists' beliefs in the creation of a new world, and in the brotherhood of man. For men, there are no purely individual activities ; everything including poetry is a social act. " La poésie doit être faite par tous et non par un " Lautréamont had said. Poetry must be accessible to every man who will find in it an inspiration. How the pure Surrealists could believe that everybody would be capable of entering their private world of images and symbols is difficult to understand. But they were at least consistent in believing that reason was the barrier between men, and thus was anti-social. There is certainly a grain of truth in that belief, but this is not the place to assess its scope. The fact remains that although the Surrealist poets wrote and published many poems in common, those who really emerged as poets of importance were those who succeeded in shaking off the dogmatism of the theorists like Breton and Tzara, who succeeded in marrying reason with unreason in a poetry which had freshness and vitality, and yet respected the traditions of order and harmony which civilization had bequeathed to man. The loss of faith in the ancient orthodoxies, the nerve-racking uncertainty of life, and the fear of complete obliteration have made people search for new prophets. Just as men have at times demanded dictatorship in politics, so they have demanded prophecy in art. The artist is expected to resume his older function of seer and to give warning of disaster. He must preach in the wilderness like St. John or speak to the wind like Cassandra, but he is generally looked at askance by the public and threatened with banishment from the City, if he writes about the mental qualms of " La Jeune Parque " instead of the miseries of the proletariat. This view seems to me a very shallow one. That poets like Aragon or Eluard succeeded in drawing inspiration from patriotism and suffering and thus inspired their fellow-men is undeniable, but the fount of inspiration can be reached by various ways, direct or indirect, easy or difficult, and those who can make the journey will discover it. Rimbaud's self-portrait, the " Cimetière Marin " or the Mona Lisa have not the same direct bearing on the events of their time as the " Liberté " of Delacroix or of Eluard, or " Guernica " of Picasso, yet who will claim that these works of art are greater than the others, that they contribute more to the glory of man and to his spiritual greatness. One group simply takes a more direct road than the other ; but there are no direct roads in art, there are only various degrees of indirectness. For if the approach is direct, the result is a statement or a copy, it is not a work of art. Each artist follows his personal bent, and it would be no more sensible and conducive to good results to ask Aragon to write " La Jeune Parque " than to ask Valéry to write " Les Yeux d'Elsa ". If such an imposition had been made upon those two writers they would either have produced the most unpoetic of poetic attempts, or, if it were poetry, it would only be what it is now under different titles. " Les Yeux d'Elsa " would have become " La Jeune Parque " and " La Jeune Parque " would have become " Les Yeux d'Elsa ". So let it be what it is, for it can only be on that condition.

Eluard's consciousness of the problems of his time, his profound preoccupation with human suffering, are genuine and express his personality. Indeed they underlie his whole poetic creation from the very early " Poèmes pour la Paix " right through " La Vie Immédiate " to his last poetry " Le rendez-vous Allemand " and " Poésie et Verité ". Few men have been more moved than Eluard by the suffering which he saw during the war. One has only to listen to him as he

describes the persecution of the Jews to realize the depth of
his sympathy.

> Je crie mon chagrin
> A faire brûler avec moi les sourds
> Et les prisonniers que le jour insulte.

But Eluard is a poet, a real poet and so in the end what
matters is not so much the value of his feelings and their
value as poetic material as the poetry itself. There is no
doubt that Eluard has written a *poésie engagée*, a poetry which
deals with problems of his time, but he has done so as a
poet who transmutes into poetry every subject that he touches.
He has succeeded because poetry is the crowning activity of
his life ; his political beliefs, his social preoccupations, his
love, the love inspired by women and by his fellow-beings,
fuse the moment into perenniality, and this timelessness only
happens in the poem, which is the end of the journey through
life and the physical world, culminating in the ideal world,
which is the poem.

I mentioned earlier, how Eluard reminded me of Maurice
Scève and I should like to return to that suggestion. For both
poets, the journey to knowledge is made by the ways of love
through the loved woman and its end is the supreme ideal
embodied in the poem. Both poets believe in searching for
and bringing out the very essence of things by starting from
the physical world, the world of the senses, and the passion
which burns in both is equally illumining. Scève is haunted
by the physical beauty of Délie as well as by the lurking presence of Death who one day might leave him naked and alone,
deprived of the source of his visionary power, his love and
his sufferings, and these compose the immortality which is
his poetry. Eluard, like Scève, shows the same absolute love
for the woman and for the world whose principle she is.
Love is for both the means of union with the world and the
sine qua non of Existence, of eternal Existence, for love is the
source of their constant rebirth out of the night of nothingness, out of the night of Time.

Ainsi passant des siècles la longueur
Surmonteras la hauteur des étoiles
Par ton saint nom, qui vis en ma langueur
Pourras partout nager à pleines voiles.

Tu es le corps, Dame, et je suis ton ombre.

And Eluard says,

Dehors nos souvenirs nuits à flancs de journée,
Agitent nos liens sans pouvoir les briser.

For Scève, Death is a transfiguration, the being which he loved has become the supreme ideal made to live again the complete life in the poem :

Car en mon corps, mon âme tu revins
Sentant ses mains, mains célestement blanches
Avec leurs bras mortellement divins
L'un couronner mon col, l'autre mes hanches.

" Aveugle aux autres ténébres, tu mourras les yeux ouverts," says Eluard.

" A poet is . . . physician to all men," said Keats in Hyperion. The sufferings of mankind are, together with the theme of Love and Death, the most important themes of Eluard's poetry. In 1918, he said :

Je fis un feu, l'azur m'ayant abandonné,
Un feu pour être son ami,
Un feu pour m'introduire dans la nuit d'hiver,

In 1939 he takes up the same poem and expounds its main theme in " Pour Vivre Ici ". His ideal, his world, is something similar to Death which has only one element, and he is

. . . le rivage et la clé
De la vie incertaine. . . .
Je suis sur terre et tout s'accommode du feu.

With his ideal, the poet, come what may, never feels alone, and in the end, the ideal which can make him forget for brief moments

La boue, le four à chaux, les trottoirs diminués

is always the woman who holds him back on the verge of the abyss.

> Qu'importe le ciel vide, je ne suis pas seul.

Throughout Eluard's poetry we find expressed, or rather suggested, the conviction that love creates Eternity, and that Time is abolished in moments of love. A poem like " Sous L'Angle d'Or " shows all Eluard's delicacy and subtlety of expression. He can make full use of an unfettered imagination bordering on fancy, and yet the tenseness of the feelings expressed is such as to make the poem rise to the heights of a pure lyrical meditation. The poet's imagination, however rich and nimble, remains within the given theme, which is sublime love.

> Lorsque nous nous regardons
> La distance s'ouvre les veines
> Le flot touche à toutes les plages.

Here we have thought expressed in sensuous images and in moving music. In fact, all the poems like " L'Absence ", and " Surgis ", which come under the heading of " Rosaces ", show the same quality as the first poem of that group, " L'Angle d'Or ". One cannot but be struck by the remarkable blend of the sensuous and the metaphysical which characterized the poetry of the sixteenth century. Indeed, the name of Maurice Scève remains present in one's mind, not because Eluard imitates him or has been influenced by him, but simply because they both believe that the poet can combine the world of ideas and the world of the senses into the transcendental form of the poem, and that this presents a world of innocence and magic, a world which brings Time back to its source.

After the " Livre Ouvert II ", which still contains many poems written in a Surrealist mood, his next book was " Le Lit La Table ", a title which suggests a poetry of everyday life, a poetry dealing with objects in an impersonal way. But with the exception of a few poems at the end, " Le Lit

La Table " is entirely devoted to the world of which Eluard
is a supreme voice, the world of love. It is a kind of closed
world which enables him to say :

> Je tiens la rue comme un verre
> Plein de lumière enchantée,

or to get lost in :

> Le contact sans fin de la nuit
> Dans les îles chaudes du cœur

Eluard continues in his own way the building of that mira-
culous cosmos based on one single word and all its complica-
tions, love.

> Années valent moins que jour
> Et la vie moins que l'année.

and it is only love which can make life :

> Faits l'un pour l'autre à tout jamais
> O toi que j'arrache à l'oubli

> O toi que j'ai voulu heureuse.
> > "Aube."

And indeed with Love it is the eternal dawn. The idea
of the dawn has a striking importance in the poetry of Eluard.
His poetry is never, or hardly ever, a poetry of assertion or
even of concrete presences and palpable objects ; his poetry
is a poetry of transparences, of absences, emerging like islands
from the tenuous liquid words which surround them and
leave room for their emergence. We seem to be constantly
on the verge of a mysterious world which only the divine
grace of love can reveal to us ; a unique dawn where we can
remain for ever as " youth unconscious of evil ". But it
is a fragile world always threatened by night, the night of
death, the night which the poet will transcend in the act of
dying, and so pass into the Eternity of his love which becomes
the poem. Eluard is one of those who believe that it is that
Eternity which brushes the shores of the subconscious where

all great poetry has its source ; thus the so-called subjectivism of the Surrealist becomes the real objectivity since it belongs to all who can reach it. But it can only be reached by the temporary abolition of Reason. The true Surrealists believed that that state could be reached by disrupting completely the logic of language by the free-wheeling of the mind ; they ended in verbalism. Eluard realizes that nothing living, reason included, can be bullied, without provoking a resistance. Reason must be coaxed into quietness and silence. That can only be done by recognizing its existence, and by gradually diminishing the logic of language, but not beyond the point where Reason will attempt to discover the lost thread and resume its favourite game of putting together the jig-saw puzzle and finding its way to the heart of the maze. In other words, Reason must always retain a very slight, very unobtrusive control over the workings of the imagination. And that is what happens with Eluard, whose poetry shines with all the colours of a vivid imagination and is at the same time luminous, practically without obscurity, and is both universal and impersonal. It is a poetry which remains extremely remote from the personal poetry of the Romantics—here Eluard is as remote as Valéry—yet every poem belongs to a world which nobody but Eluard could have built. We cannot fail to recognize its origins.

But we must not forget that, with the desire to create a pure impersonal poetry, Eluard was deeply moved by the events and troubles of the world in which he lived. The last poems of " Le Lit La Table " show once more his awareness of human suffering. Poems like " Jungle ", " Le Monde est Nul ", " Le Cimetière des Fous " are amongst the most moving poems of our time, and remain unsurpassed in their poignant description of madness. Above all there is " Le Rendez-vous Allemand ", Eluard's war poems, poems in which not only did he completely depart from his former rather impersonal poetry but in which he took the trouble to describe some of the events which gave birth to the poems. Yet these poems, which are amongst the most moving to be written during the war, transcend the event which inspired them. Poems like "Sept Poèmes d'Amour en Guerre", "Critique de la Poésie", "Les Armes de la Douleur", or "Enterrar Y Callar", "Pensez", are poems of extreme tension which have gained from their localization in time and space the pathos which makes them unforgettable. Here we can see how the myth rises from the event through the medium of poetry. Eluard is not only able to make poetry out of the event, he can also write philosophical poetry. "Vue donne Vie" expresses a belief common today that nothing lives without man.

> Sœurs miroitières de mes larmes
> Les étoiles brillaient autour de ma fenêtre
> Et mes yeux refermant leurs ailes pour la nuit
> Vivaient d'un univers sans bornes.
>
> . . . .
>
> Je sais le sort de la lumière
> J'en ai assez pour jouer son éclat
> Pour me parfaire au dos de mes paupières
> Pour que rien ne vive sans moi.

Other poems which express Eluard's conception of life are "Mes Heures":

> Je fus homme je fus rocher
> Je fus rocher dans l'homme homme dans le rocher
> Je fus oiseau dans l'air espace dans l'oiseau
> Je fus fleur dans le froid fleuve dans le soleil
> Escarboucle dans la rosée
>
> Fraternellement seul fraternellement libre.

and "Marines" which begins with these beautiful lines:

> Je me suis pris à caresser
> La mer qui hume les orages.
>
> Ma bouche au ras des flots buveuse de paroles
> Prenant l'or au soleil sur un chemin d'or chaud.

The last poem of Eluard is "Poésie Ininterrompue" which is a Surrealist poem, but it is a Surrealism personal to Eluard.

Here we have probably the best example of that power to suggest the absent object. The words shape the object and the hollow it must fill. They are words which at times have no weight and seem to efface themselves from the page ; they simply give a flame which lights up the next word and then disappears and the trail of fire lights up the form of the living thing which is the poem and which becomes part of our experience. The beginning of the poem is composed of an amazing series of adjectives without substantives, a process which consists in surrounding the thing without ever naming it, using the words as Mallarmé used them sometimes, not in order to name the thing but in order to destroy the real object which they represent, so that all that remains is the hollow which contained the object and the object itself becomes more real by its absence than by its presence. Eluard applies this method with consummate success in " Poésie Ininterrompue ". The light transparent words of the beginning

> Nue effacée ensommeillée
> Choisie sublime solitaire
>
> .   .   .   .   .
>
> Froide nacrée ébouriffée
> Fidèle facile étoilée.

are soon replaced by the heavy, dark, opaque words which suggest the idea that light has transformed itself into darkness, the night of the self which the poet is going to explore. Or rather, he will open the doors and allow the self to emerge and unfold its mysterious aspects.

" Poésie Ininterrompue " is a succession of autobiographical soliloquies by the poet and the loved woman. Their meditations are so entangled that the whole poem appears to be a kind of day dream in which consciousness yet plays a tenuous part since the poem has a philosophical drift. The drift is at times difficult to follow and in spite of impressively successful passages, these are too disconnected. There are not only many successive themes, but the poem raises a number of conceptual problems, and therefore the lack of a single pattern makes the reader too anxious to find the missing links. It excites the reason and inhibits the state of expectation and perfect receptivity which is necessary before the poetic experience can be born. The philosophy is that which we are accustomed to find in Eluard's poetry. The central symbol is the loved woman :

> C'est par toi que je parle et tu restes au centre du tout.

and through the woman Eluard reaches once more the beliefs which are his and which are fairly close to the main tenets of existentialist philosophy.

> Pas de regrets j'ignore tout d'hier
> Aujourd'hui lumière unique
> Aujourd'hui l'enfance entière
> Changeant la vie en lumière
> Sans passé sans lendemain.
>
> . . . . .
>
> Aujourd'hui rêve de nuit
> Au grand jour tout se lève
> Aujourd'hui je suis toujours.

Once more we find the idea of perfect love reducing Time to the eternal present :

> Tous les morts nous ressemblent
> Tous les morts que nous aimions
> Les autres sont imaginaires
>
> . . . . .
>
> Un cœur seul pas de cœur
> Un seul cœur tous les cœurs.

says Eluard, summing up once more his supreme belief in love, in a phrase which comes as near to punning as possible. But a poet must love words. The love of words quite often leads Shakespeare to puns which are out of place. The love of words in " Poésie Ininterrompue " manifests itself in a pure verbalism which in a few instances seems to be the only link between the consecutive meditations. Yet the poem

L

has enough passages of moving beauty to be given an important place in the poetry of Eluard.

Our emotions radiate upon the cosmos in which we live, and this in turn lives in us and with us. The poet echoes the interplay of these sounds ; he is the central vision, source and reflection, the clearest expression of the self. The universal self speaks through him, and he then becomes man, sole witness to the existence of God and the cosmos. Thus the poet can be subjective and impersonal in the highest degree, and this is the case with Eluard whose poetry is for everybody, and by everybody, for the poet is the voice of all those silent ones who feel dimly but cannot speak.

> Je parle pour les quelques hommes qui se taisent
> Les meilleurs.
> > "L'Amour la Poésie."

All poetic experience, all search for the mysterious truth beyond reason and the senses is an arduous journey, " a season in hell ", as Rimbaud called it, a journey to the underworld like that of Orpheus, the prince of poets, or across the desert like that of St. John, the herald of Christ. But the journey towards the truth which lies in the depth of the self and is the truth of the cosmos must be barren of result unless the search is made with a mediator who is one of the symbols of mankind ; Eurydice, Beatrice, Marguerite, and, on the highest level, Christ and the Blessed Virgin, are all symbolic figures interposed between God and Man. If we make the search unaccompanied, we are liable to self-destruction, like Hölderlin or Gérard de Nerval.

For Eluard, the mediator, the source of Life and Eternity, the shield which shelters him from Time, is the woman, complement of man and the womb of life. The greater part of Eluard's poetry is a dialogue between him and the loved woman, or a meditation on the woman who is love. In that very human and yet transcendental love—for it embraces the earth, life itself, and becomes the source of eternity—there is no mention of Divinity. The " I and

Thou " dialogue is between man and woman in Time, combining into " the one " which transcends Time.   Life begins with the loved one

> Et si je ne sais plus tout ce que j'ai vécu
> C'est que tes yeux ne m'ont pas toujours vu.
>   " Capitale de la Douleur."

With her it is always the dawn of a world ever new emerging from the night, the night in which the poet had to plunge, like Orpheus, to find his Love.   The loved one waited for the necessary complement to make the timeless present without past or future, in which the world only exists in relation to the poet and his love.   The poet becomes the centre and source of the universe, the sun which makes life.   Like the sun, his warmth and light do not exist unless they are reflected ; but however different the parts played by the earth the sun and the other planets or by man and woman, their importance is equal, for Light and Love require the presence of both in order to exist.   The woman is the mirror ; in her, in her face, in her eyes, the poet sees himself and the world reflected, and through her he shares in the sufferings of men and in the infinite life of the universe.

> Il fallait bien qu'un visage
> Réponde à tous les noms du monde.
>   " L'Amour la Poésie."

The symbols of night, light, the sun, the mirror, continuously recur in Eluard's poetry.   It is a poetry essentially humane, ethereal, anthropomorphic ; a poetry in which the here and now are at the source of the transcendental experience which is the poem,

> Je vis ce rêve entre les flammes
> Entre les griffes du soleil
> Et sur mon corps ton corps étend
> La nappe de son miroir clair.
>   " Une Longue Réflexion Amoureuse."

It is a poetry without metaphysical anxieties.   The idea of sin does not exist ; night is not the night of Baudelaire, nor the night of Hugo. It is the night which the sun-love dispels. The *Angst* of Kierkegaard, the " Creux toujours futur " of Valéry or of the existentialists are unknown to Eluard. His poetry is the poetry of the moment, the point around which everything centres. His poetic images follow the pattern of his life ; they do not unfold along a kind of imaginary line ; on the contrary, they revolve round a central point which continually creates them and to which they consistently return. It is not unlike the poetic " method " of Dylan Thomas. I once compared this to a playing fountain with a central jet ; the same image applies to Eluard's poetry, whose aim it is to convey the timeless experience born from Love. Without Love, the self continuously endeavouring to reach the absolute through absolute knowledge, would devour itself and compel the death of the self by the suicide of the body. Eluard has been brought face to face with that terrible image of death by the tragic disappearance of the love which formed the reality in which he lived, and which protected him from the dread of Death. What will be the outcome of this sudden tearing of the veil, which has left the poet standing on the brink of the abyss ? Immense suffering, certainly, but what will be the result in poetry ? The most Orphic lyricism, or a flight towards the Shakespearian heights from which man confronts his fate, steadfastly, and resolves himself into it, into the Eternal ?

NOTE

This book was completed at the beginning of the year 1948. Since then, Eluard has published other books, including a volume entitled " Poèmes Politiques ", with a remarkable preface by Aragon. That preface, fired with Aragon's convictions, is not only an interesting literary document, but also a sincere and very moving tribute from one poet to another. Strangely enough, it talks about that " season in hell " mentioned earlier in the course of this essay, and, what is more, seems to confirm its conclusions. For, as Aragon says, for Eluard the marriage of Heaven and Hell is not beyond, but in life ; the Journey through Hell of Eluard is neither metaphysical nor æsthetic, but essentially human : it takes place in the whole man—through his flesh and soul ; and indeed, when Eluard returns and accepts life, it is not to fill lonely vales with the melancholy sound of his lute, nor to seek exhaustion on the hot sands of Ethiopia, but to help other men to live, " to give them hope which they badly need, in spite of the robust joys of love ".

I feel at one with Aragon on that point, and I have only to conjure up Eluard's strongly moved face, while he was describing the horrors which he had seen during this war, or his anxiety about the Spanish war, and about the apathy which prevailed all round while the shadows lengthened over Europe, to be made fully aware of his strong sense of responsibility and of his belief that the poet must be, first and foremost, the consciousness of his age and the voice which can speak for the countless silent sufferers.

The anxious question which concluded the essay on Eluard seems for me to have been answered. His poetry bears both the mark of an Orphic lyricism and also a spark of the Shakespearian mastery in resolving contrasts and in contemplating steadfastly man's fate, not on the Shakespearian plane of cosmic forces and mysteries which plunge deep down into the very sources of life, but, on the contrary, rooted in the historical context of living here and now, in a brotherhood of suffering and hope :

> Vivre c'est partager, je hais la solitude
>
> . . . .
>
> Le seul abri possible c'est le monde entier
>
> . . . .
>
> Vivre se perdre afin de retrouver les hommes.

Eluard's latest poetry seems to me to confirm two aspects of his poetic genius—the purely lyrical and the social, or, rather, the human aspect of his poetry. Eluard has succeeded

in integrating in his poetry his social and political views. He
has succeeded where so many poets of our time who tried to
do the same thing have failed, because his love of his fellow-
beings is not sectarian, as that of Aragon can sometimes be,
and also because it is deep-rooted enough to exclude that
attitude of apparent detachment and light cynicism which
mars some of Auden's poetry.

Poems like " Sœurs d'espérance ", " Aujourd'hui ", or
" Dit de la force de l'amour ", show that Eluard can transmute
his ideas and feelings about men and their ways of life into
a substance which lives like flesh and blood and which bears
the marks of a poet who is obviously endowed with a very
rare sensitiveness. In short, if Eluard succeeds where others
failed, it is because he loves men as persons and not as groups
or historical concepts, and because he speaks about them as
a man who is profoundly and sincerely moved by the suffering
which he has experienced and not as the mouthpiece of the
historical forces which he expresses. These remarks point
to what is Eluard's most distinctive and greatest gift—the
gift of lyricism, a gift which seems to me to be the most
remarkable of our time. Few poets have ever succeeded in
expressing as poignantly, as movingly, as he has done, the
hollowness and yet the harrowing presence of absence :

> Morte visible Nusch invisible et plus dure
> Que la soif et la faim a mon corps épuisé
> Masque de neige sur la terre et sous la terre
> Source des larmes dans la nuit masque d'aveugle
> Mon passé se dissout je fais place au silence.
> "Le Temps Déborde."

Few poets have succeeded in conveying as movingly and
as penetratingly as Eluard the experience of love, half-dead,
half-living, decaying under the earth and yet burning with
life through the senses, the eyes and the hands of the one
who has remained behind :

> Noir c'est mon nom quand je m'éveille
> Noir le singe qui me tracasse

Qui grimace moule à manies
Devant le miroir de ma nuit
Noir c'est mon poids de déraison
C'est ma moitié froide pourrie

. . . .

J'étais construit les mains ensemble
Doublé de deux mains dans les miennes
J'étais construit avec deux yeux
Qui se chargeaient des miens pour voir
Mais aujourd'hui je sens mes os
Se fendre sous le froid parfait

Je sens le monde disparaître
Rien ne demeure de nos rires
Ni de nos nuits ni de nos rêves
Et la rosée est charbonneuse
J'ai trop pleuré la coque est vide
Où nous ne pouvions qu'être deux.

"Poèmes Politiques."

Those last poems of Eluard bring to mind the poetry of
Donne, and Donne's name shines with a light which, if it
does not illumine vast oceans and continents, has for the
human heart a glow more moving and more lasting than
many more far-reaching rays.

VII

ST. JOHN PERSE AND HENRI MICHAUX

IT is always arbitrary to attempt to bring together various writers into well-arranged groups. Yet since reasoning thrives on simplification and generalization, literary criticism, which is above all an attempt to rationalize about art, naturally tends to work towards groupings. That process makes the task of the critic easier, but there are writers who cannot be fitted into any movement, into any group, and seem to have neither forebears nor followers. St. John Perse and Michaux belong to this category.

St. John Perse's poetry is said to be difficult, and indeed it is so, for anyone who tries to discover in it the logical meaning of a direct statement. St. John Perse's poetry is a kind of spoken meditation, in the course of which the poet follows the drift of his splendid imagination, unfolding scenes, landscapes, and thoughts according to the law which presides over his affective life. The meditation is presented to us in grave sustained rhythms reminiscent at times of Claudel's *verset*, and within the context of a theme. For, however close to Surrealism St. John Perse might appear to be, he himself has stated " Je m'éleverai toujours contre l'activité du songe ", and he believes in the control of the mind. If we take a remarkable poem like " Pluies " for instance, we shall at once realize that that poem, with its mysterious symbolism, its subtle blend of the real world with the world beyond the senses, its constant awareness of the continuous presence of past and future in the consciousness of the poet, which seems to be the consciousness of man in the cosmos —we shall discover in all this a magic and splendour which increase with each reading. Beautiful lines like : " Nous n'en finirons pas de voir trainer sur l'étendue des mers la

153

fumée des hauts faits où charbonne l'histoire ", are juxtaposed with phrases like " Ce soir logera chez l'habitant, ou les catafalques du Habsbourg ". These remind us that in spite of his seeming remoteness and his attempt to shelter behind an extremely subtle diction, the poet is a twentieth-century man and that the rains are more than ever necessary in our time of biblical wrath.

Vous, laveuses des morts dans les eaux-mères du matin—et c'est la terre encore aux ronces de la guerre—lavez aussi la face des vivants ; lavez, ô Pluies ! la face triste des violents, la face douce des violents . . . car leurs voies sont étroites, et leurs demeures incertaines.

and the rains become the divine pardon which will cleanse the memory and permit the return of man to his essence.

La nuit venue, les grilles closes, que pèse l'eau du ciel au bas-empire des taillis ?

A la pointe des lances le plus clair de mon bien ! . . . Et toutes choses égales au fléau de l'esprit,

Seigneur terrible de mon rire, vous porterez ce soir l'esclandre au plus haut lieu.

. . . Car telles sont vos délices, Seigneur, au seuil aride du poème, où mon rire épouvante les paons verts de la gloire.

What is the weight of divine mercy? All things are equal in the scales of the mind, said Valéry. St. John Perse says the same thing. And God will witness once more the hopeless attempts of the poet who will not derive any glory from the poem. Good poetry defies analysis and always retains its mysterious core which cannot be penetrated, but which is a never-failing source of poetic enjoyment for those who can reach it. The impenetrable core of St. John Perse's poetry might be larger than usual, yet the core is there, soaked in poetry, flowing forth with each successive wave of reading, like those porous stones which take centuries to liberate slowly the moisture which they have gathered throughout the ages.

Another poet whom one cannot link up with any tradition or group is Henri Michaux. Michaux is above all a witness of his time ; caught between the ever-threatening pincers of awe-inspiring nothingness and of cruel merciless reality, he is driven to obsessions and to paralysis in face of the dangers which threaten him. Which one will he face up to ? The oppressive presence of an existing reality or the dreaded vacuum of nothingness. What can he do but seek refuge in a masochism which impels him to minute descriptions of the obsessions and the sufferings which form the matter of his poetry. Michaux, like his hero and mouthpiece " Plume ", is the plaything of an absurd universe, and he only frees himself from the weight of the incredible mishaps and miseries which afflict him by laughter. However tense a situation might be, a wild burst of laughter will break the tenseness. Michaux like Kafka is constantly bullied by the Law ; indeed, both share in the feeling of inborn guilt. " Plume " like " Joseph K——" lives in a world which is not his own, hence the acceptance of the idea that he may be guilty of anything. " Il fut bientôt évident (dès mon adolescence) que j'étais né pour vivre parmi les monstres." Monsters haunt Michaux's life, and literally become his life, as he says in the poem " Le Lobe à Monstres ". Michaux like Kafka finds that he is a stranger on earth but unlike Kafka, he reacts against the law and frees himself from it by a more savage laughter than that of the Black Dean or the author of " Candide ". " La difficulté est d'être douce à la fois et de serrer fort ", he says in " Voyage en Grande Garabagne " about the young girl employed in killing those who breathe with difficulty. He certainly is an authentic rebel if there has ever been one in literature. He rebels against reality which he finds absurd and evil, but above all, he is probably a rebel for rebellion's sake. There is in him a constant refusal of acceptance, of being something, and he tries to make up for this lack by his poetry, but he himself is unable to define the source of his longings.

Tournant le dos, je partis, je ne dis rien, j'avais la mer en moi,
la mer éternellement autour de moi.

Quelle mer ?   Voilà ce que je serais bien empêché de préciser.
"La Mer."

In order to destroy reality he began by attempting to
destroy language or rather by attempting to empty the words
of their meaning. Poems like " Le Grand Combat " and
" Saouls " from " Qui je fus ", or " L'Avenir " from " Mes
Propriétés ", begin with words which do not exist and are
intermingled or end with words which exist, but whose
contiguity with non-existent words deprives them of their
meaning and prompts the final conclusion that life is nonsense.
The result is bewildering, amusing at times, but not convincing, and far less entertaining than his straightforward non-
sensical descriptions of strange countries or of the extraordinary life of " Plume ".   One must also note that though
Michaux writes at times in a Surrealist vein, not only did
he never belong to the Surrealist group but he was at the
opposite pole from their aims ; for if the Surrealists sought
to break language in order to use it as signs or symbols of
a hidden reality, Michaux' nihilism is purely gratuitous and
does not attempt to reveal any mystery.   For him, poetry
is a medicine, a cure for his obsessions ; he exorcizes himself
by his creative art.   Instead of letting the monster grow in
himself as in " La Vie Double " he objectifies it in the poem
which by its existence liberates and relieves him.   In " La
Vie Double " he says that all the ideas and sentiments which
we discard because they are alien to us or because they are
too close to other ideas which we accept, go to form an entity
which lives in us, grows with our daily rejections and acquires
greater and greater possibilities of destruction. Aware of
that danger, we hope to avoid it by trying to assimilate
instead of discarding the elements which are destructive to
us.   In order to avoid obsessions one must exorcize oneself
by writing or by any other kind of artistic expression.   In
the preface to " Epreuves, Exorcismes ", he says : " For the

one who understands, the poems at the beginning of this
book have not been written out of hatred of this or that,
but in order to relieve obsessions. Most of the texts which
follow are a kind of cunning exorcism. Their *raison d'être*
is to keep at bay the surrounding powers of the hostile world."
But he said somewhere else : " Poetry is a gift of Nature, a
gift and not work, the very desire to write a poem is sufficient
to kill it " ; and further on he adds : " One writes only
out of necessity, to liberate oneself for a moment, in the end
to write is a weakness, for as soon as one attempts to write
one betrays what is best in us. One should keep everything
for oneself." This is very reminiscent of Monsieur Teste,
stained by the expression which broke his state of pure
possibility and made him known ; and Valéry was not alone
in having felt the terror of giving expression, which is also
in a way the terror of the white page. Rimbaud and
Mallarmé keep him company.

Life must oscillate between the centrifugal forces of anarchy
and the centripetal forces of union in order to continue in
the best conditions. Michaux is torn by those conflicting
principles. He tries to be " one " and nothingness obsesses
him, but he never knows who he is, who speaks in him ;
he is inhabited by hundreds of voices and with great pathos,
he tells of weird monsters taking possession of his life. Is
he a monster, a river or an apple, or other things ? He does
not know, he is everything in turn :

> Partir est peu commode et de même l'expliquer.
>
> Mais en un mot, je puis vous le dire. Souffrir est le mot.
> Quand j'arrivai dans la pomme, j'étais glacé !

Michaux believes only in subjective reality ; he refuses to
accept anything which is not his personal experience. What
he feels seems to him beyond communication and he finds
the words lame, incomplete, and incapable of expressing the
complexities of the human heart. Language is by definition
simplification in order to render objective and apprehensible
by all, what is most subjective in us, and Michaux thinks that

gestures, sounds, and colours are more expressive than words. The painter has more direct contacts with the outside world, and more direct means of expressing it than the writer.

Michaux is first and foremost a prose writer, but he reaches the tenseness and the emotion of poetry in his poems or prose-writings of the volume " Epreuves, Exorcismes ". This, to my mind, is his best work. There we find, in writings, which have no trace of Surrealist verbosity or obscurity (for Michaux is very artful, very precise, as is shown in the poem " Il Ecrit ", whose implication is that writing requires the unfailing attention and supreme technical skill of the surgeon), the very moving experiences of a man who, obsessed by feelings of guilt and impotence, rises from the personal to the general and presents to us the tragedy of man. " Ecce Homo " is the title of one of his best and most moving poems and could be the title of the volume which contains it. Here is man with his harrowing insight into his consciousness, with his agonies in the middle of alien sullen reality, man condemned to watch helplessly the development of his demonic skill which, matched with his suicidal tendencies, will reduce mankind to nothingness. Where can one seek refuge? In concrete things, in the world beyond? No-where—and the poet describes with a child-like intuition the plight of his age.

Etions-nous nés pour la gangue?
Etions-nous nés, doigts cassés, pour donner toute une vie à un mauvais problème?

or the plight of man in the moving poem " Voix " with its splendid ending, reminiscent of Pascal

Celui qu'un caillou fait trébucher marchait déjà depuis deux cent mille ans quand j'entendis les voix de haine et de menaces, qui prétendaient lui faire peur.

It is difficult to find anything more moving and yet more torn by ferocious humour than the poems " J'ai vu " or " Ecce Homo ".

Je n'ai pas vu l'homme recueilli, méditant sur son être admirable. Mais j'ai vu l'homme recueilli comme un crocodile qui de ses yeux de glace regarde venir sa proie et en effet il l'attendait bien protégé au bout d'un fusil long. Cependant les obus tombant autout de lui étaient encore beaucoup mieux protégés. Ils avaient une coiffe à leur bout qui avait été spécialement étudiée pour sa dureté, pour sa dureté implacable.

and the conclusion of the poem

Et c'était la paix, la paix assurément, un jour, bientôt, la paix comme il y en eut déjà des millions, une paix d'hommes, une paix qui n'obturerait rien.

Voici que la paix s'avance semblable à un basset pleurétique et l'homme planckton, l'homme plus nombreux que jamais, l'homme un instant excédé, qui attend toujours et voudrait un peu de lumière . . .

Most poems of " Epreuves, Exorcismes " are good but one cannot talk of that book without mentioning the very remarkable group of poems called " La Marche dans le Tunnel ". The symbolism of the title is clear enough and after having dealt in the first part with the *petitesse de l'homme* in lashing ironical terms, the poet comes to our age, and, in rhythms and images reminiscent of the Bible, unfolds the litany, in turn melancholy or passionate, which the tragic suffering of man prompts to his heart :

Les idées, comme des boucs étaient dressées les unes contre les autres. La haine prenait une allure sanitaire. La vieillesse faisait rire et l'enfant fut poussé à mordre. Le monde était tout drapeau.

. . . .

Des peuples, les uns gagnaient, les autres crevaient, mais tous restaient emmêlés dans une misère qui faisait le tour de la Terre.

Then the suffering of the occupied countries :

Il fallait un permis pour recevoir une bouchée de pain.

Une pomme trouvée dans la terre était plus entourée qu'un proche parent, and the twelfth passage describing France :

> En ce temps-là un grand pays se trouva comme un pays petit.
>
> En ce temps-là celui qui avait jeté tant de lumière fut en grande obscurité,

And the last poem of the group, unfinished :

> Où vas-tu homme à la tripe lâche ?
> L'homme va dans sa grange à idées. Cette idée le tuera.
> N'importe, il faut qu'il y aille.

" La grange à idées " will be the end of man. Never has such a remark seemed more pregnant with truth. Man strides towards discoveries more and more dangerous, and many are those who like Michaux feel that the " grange à idées " will prove to be the end of man. Michaux speaks for his age and the importance of his artistic creations resides not so much in their intrinsic artistic value, as in their perfect embodiment and expression of the fateful hour in which we live.

CONCLUSION

LITERATURE is an emanation of life and as such cannot be cut into separate sections. To be felt and appreciated, it must always be viewed as a living whole as old as social man, and older than he is in its essence. Ideas do not know any frontiers in space or time. The ideas of Plato are present in our time just as the ideas of our time were present in Plato's time. It is not because we do not see some of Plato's ideas or because some of our ideas were not seen in Plato's time that those ideas did not exist. It would be the same as denying the existence of the Himalaya mountains because one has not seen them. Plato was looking at things from Greece nearly 2,500 years ago. We are looking from another stage in time and space, but we are looking at the same things and the difference of view is due to the difference of position. If these things were looked at from Mars, or from some even more remote distance, from Eternity, they would have the same appearance because they do not change. They are the essentials and thus are eternal. Just as there is a difference between digging the ground with a pick-axe and with an electric machine, in the same way there is a difference, if the search for these essentials is made at different times and with different implements, which are the words ; but these differences are superficial and are only interpretations of essences which are eternal. Philosophical systems come and go, shifting the emphasis from one aspect to another, but the fundamental source of philosophy, which is life, remains unchanged because it is a manifestation of eternity and returns to it. Philosophers can argue whether existence precedes essence or vice versa, the fundamental fact is that existence is essence and that essence is only revealed, and therefore is, through existence, so that one cannot separate one from the other, or establish an order of precedence. They are simultaneous. Poetry which is the search for the hidden reality or the attempt to create that eternal reality through existence is an essence which transcends time and space so that the intuitive flights of Plato rejoin the mystical world of Blake or Mallarmé. The universalism of Goethe is also that of Leonardo da Vinci and Valéry's transcendentalism recalls that of Maurice Scève.

Poetry is by nature indefinable. Each poet reaches his own poetic world by his own ways and the very essence of poetry lies in the innermost depth of the poet's self, beyond consciousness, in a world in which all genuine poets meet. But the fact remains that those mysterious experiences called poetry are embodied in language, live beyond the separate meaning of words by the magic of rhythm, and have a life which springs from the whole. In fact the poem, in its final form of words, is the only thing that remains of the mystery which is the poetic experience—the words ready to be burnt in order to produce for each reader the light, the words which are the key to the unfathomable mystery, the words and nothing else. In the end the poem is language. This means that writers writing in the same language are bound to have something in common, for they use the same words with certain generally accepted associations, with an atmosphere and a history which are those of the country in which the words live and which the words describe. The French language is France with her history, her landscapes, her characteristic traits, her traditions, and her literature.

Every poet of importance affects the whole literature, past and future, of the language in which he writes, for he is at the same time a manifestation of that literature and a landmark which can be neither repeated nor altered. Therefore, it seems to me impossible to attempt to describe some of the traits of any given period of literature without attempting to link that period with the one which preceded. It seems beyond question that to try to find traits shared by a group

of writers like Scève, Racine, and Claudel, or by another
group of writers like Shakespeare, Browning, and Eliot,
would not only be an impossible, but also a fruitless, task;
yet at the same time it remains true to say that each one
of those two groups of writers has a common denominator
which is the language which it uses.

Poetry is language, passionate language, and as such it
shows some of the qualities and failings of the language which
contains it. The English language, because of its subtleness,
fluidity, malleability, and richness of imagery and metaphor,
is probably the most poetic of living languages. Those assets
are reflected in the body of English poetry, which has a
very wide musical range, varying from the alliterative
rhythms of Langland, the Shakespearian and Miltonic blank
verse, to the contrapuntal melodies of Hopkins and the subtle
music of Eliot. If I were asked to single out one quality
as being the dominant force in English poetry, I should say
—imagination, and I do not mean fancy or "fantaisie", I
mean the creative power which underlies the great syntheses
of Shakespeare, Milton, or Racine, that very same power
which enabled Dante to span the mysterious universe from
the depths of the "Inferno" to the pure light of "Paradiso".
The Scots language for instance, could be considered as one
of the English languages, yet it is different enough from
English to show in its poetry the very qualities and defects
which constitute its individuality. Scots poetry is satirical,
humorous, descriptive, vigorous, realistic, fantastic, but
neither imaginative nor mystical, neither greatly rich in
image nor in metaphor. On the whole, these are the very
salient traits of the Scots language, which is robust, direct,
highly expressive in an onomatopœic way, but, like the
French, rather poor in image and metaphor. Imagination
is not the main quality of Scottish poetry, whose purest
lyricism is to be found in the ballads, which are the high-
water mark of that poetry, and in the songs of Burns and
Hugh McDiarmid. The French genius is closer to the Scots
than to the English. The French language is also closer to

M*

the Scots than to the English—it is analytical rather than
synthetic, not easy to handle, rather stiff, and far from possess-
ing the wealth of images and sounds of the English language.
The result is that rhetoric plays a far more important part in
French than in English ; French poetry on the whole reflects
those traits.

I have tried to lay stress upon the fact that poetry, being
language, cannot fail to exhibit certain characteristics of the
language which contains it, and at the same time I have
insisted on the perennial quality of the main themes of poetry
which like Life transcend national frontiers and historical
Time.   Now more than ever before, the world is consciously
one ; the joys and disappointments which men undergo in
one part of the earth affect the rest of mankind ; the poetry
of Mayakovski is echoed by that of Aragon and others, and
I do not see how one can ever attempt to reach certain
conclusions by confining an examination of poetry, to one
country only.   That is why in these notes towards a conclusion I shall try to widen my field of observation, and
I shall try to look at poetry within the wider context of
Western European society with special references to the
poetry I know best—English and French poetry.

Before attempting to express what can only be very personal views about possible developments in poetry, I should
like to try to circumscribe the area of unavoidable disagreement
by saying a few words about the terms Romanticism and
Classicism.   These two aspects of artistic expression have
always been present side by side, yet with alternating degrees
of pre-eminence, enabling us to speak, and with reason, of
a Classical or Romantic age.   The age of Virgil, for instance,
or that of Dryden was, on the whole, Classical ; the age of
the Renaissance or the age of Lamartine and Shelley was,
on the whole, Romantic.   In fact, we can see at once that
the words " Classic " and " Romantic " only have their full
meaning when used historically.   When it comes to individuals, the problem is different and beyond solution.   Indeed,
what was Shakespeare, a Classic or a Romantic ?   He was

neither, he was something more ; he was Shakespeare. And
what about Dante ; was he a Romantic—a great innovator in
form, a lonely explorer of the depths of the soul ? He was all
that, but he was Dante ; and no definition can contain him.
What about Milton, who scattered through his great work
allusions to Greek and Roman mythology, who used those
same allegories and symbols which form the basis of what
is described as Classical literature, and at the same time is
responsible for the creation of that great rebel Satan—proto-
type of all Romantic heroes from those of Goethe to those
of Byron and Chateaubriand ? And is Racine's Phèdre less
passionate, less absorbed by her emotions than any Romantic
hero whether he is called Manfred or René ? Certainly not,
but the difference is, that although Phèdre could only be born
from the mind and heart of Racine, she remains Phèdre—
an objective creation who has a life of her own, while René
or Manfred are merely the voices of Chateaubriand or Byron.

I am rather inclined to think that the classification into
" Romantic " and " Classic ", taken out of any historical
context, only acquires a semblance of justification if one deals
with extremes or with the pejorative meanings of the two
words. Good examples of Classicism are Racine, Boileau,
Pope, and Dryden. It seems to me that enough has been
said about Racine to show that he is above classification.
As for Pope, Dryden, and Boileau, who, on the whole, allow
a greater pre-eminence to intellect than to emotion, their
greatest achievements are the poems in which they have
discarded that division, and fused thought and feeling into
a poetry of wit which has reconciled contrasts and has an
emotional oneness.

It is wise to remember that very often the word " Classic "
has been reduced to meaning merely abstract, dried up poetry,
while the word " Romantic " has come to mean sentimental,
escapist, or incapable of standing irony. Other attempts at
drawing up differences between Classic and Romantic resolve
themselves into the difference between form and content.
Romantic art is supposed to create its own form, while

Classical art is supposed to adapt content to a given structure. It seems to me that this separation between form and content is highly artificial. The work of art is first and foremost the form, which becomes significant as a living thing containing, intricately woven, content and form, the content only existing in the form expressed. "That which is creative must create itself," said Keats. Byron or Keats did not invent, or rather were not the first to write in the verseforms or stanzas which they used, neither did Racine invent the alexandrine. Besides that, some of Keats' odes are as perfect in form as any of Pope's or Dryden's poems ; the same perfection of form is found in Donne, who preceded the Classical age. In fact, it is difficult to discuss that separation between form and content in poetry without becoming involved in a discussion on the very nature of poetry. Indeed, when such a separation exists the result is not poetry ; for although one might extract a rational meaning from the words of a poem, the poem is, as Eliot said, "not what it says, but what it is". If some of Shelley's or Hugo's poetry fails as poetry, it is because the poet tends at times to state his beliefs merely adorned with beautiful images. Beauty then becomes ancillary to the beliefs of the poet. Keats generally succeeds in avoiding that error ; he avoids didacticism and its oversimplifications, and he does not use the poetic experience as an object to be beautified but as having an intrinsic value. Shelley and Hugo, at times, use imagery in order to prepare us for the vague abstractions which are their thoughts and beliefs ; the result is bad poetry or no poetry. When Keats does that, as in his "Ode to a Grecian Urn", he does it successfully. There the generalization is a normal development of the emotions underlying the poem.

In poetry, the thought is the image or symbol fused in an inseparable way, as they are in good metaphysical or Symbolist poetry. In Romantic poetry, the separation between content and form has been too often apparent, and that to the detriment of poetry. The Romantic age was an age of upheavals and enthusiasm, an age where poets held

passionate beliefs and were inclined to think with Shelley
that they were the "unacknowledged legislators of mankind". They tended to moralize and to preach in a very
personal way, that is, speaking in the first person, for of
course everybody, Classic or Romantic, directly or indirectly,
can only speak of himself. They took themselves very
seriously, and confused generalizations with imaginative insight. They wore their hearts on their sleeves, they haunted
graveyards and believed with Musset that "Rien ne nous
rend si grand qu'une grande douleur", or that "L'homme
est un apprenti, la douleur est son maître."

The growth of science in the middle of the nineteenth
century partly dispelled the legendary sources of Romanticism,
shook its religious background and introduced a sense of
realism and universalism in the arts. That does not mean
that no traces of Romanticism were to be found in the artistic
creations of the 1860's ; far from it. There are no absolute
deaths in life, there are only transformations. Madame
Bovary and Salâmmbo are the alternatives to "Bouvard et
Pecuchet". The philosophical generalizations of Tennyson
or Browning, the impersonal creations of the believers in
'art for art's sake', brought about the epoch-making poetry
of Hopkins and a return to subjectivity in the arts known
as Symbolism. Symbolism, with its mixture of the real and
the imaginary, its imprecision akin to music, the interdependence of the senses, and its attempts to communicate personal experience in personal symbols and images, succeeds in
bringing together Romantic and Metaphysical poetry. The
best examples of that blend are Baudelaire, Mallarmé, and
W. B. Yeats. The latter shows in his own work the transition
from the serious Romantic poetry of his youth to the metaphysical Symbolism of his very impressive later poetry, a
poetry which proves that he had mastered all the conflicting
and opposed elements of a fluctuating personality and by
the power of his imagination, fused them into poetic creations.
A kind of similar development can be traced in Eliot, who,
although he is far from the Romanticism of Yeats, passed

from the romantic Symbolism of his early poetry to the supreme synthesis of all genres, which constitutes his great achievements from the "Waste Land" onwards. Both Eliot and Yeats stress the vital importance of suffering ; for Eliot death is the door to life, and out of suffering comes poetry ; Yeats insists on the importance of conflict and suffering which form the intense moments, the only moments when one lives ; here we have what would be described now as an existential attitude, but it was also a Romantic attitude.

Now we are living in an age of upheavals and destruction of beliefs ; " things fall apart, the centre is nowhere ", as Yeats said. The Romantic era was an era of upheavals but also an era of beliefs ; therefore the artist could be serious, serious to the point of being ridiculous. Now that beliefs are at a low ebb, the artist cannot be so serious ; he is too self-conscious, too afraid of being ridiculous, and he feels an exile in the society which gave him birth and which has outgrown him. The result is that he can hardly avoid being essentially introvert and subjective. He may, like Michaux, feel obsessed by the absurdity of life ; he may try to have that feeling of integration in the society in which he lives by being, like Auden, Spender, or Aragon, the expression of a social consciousness ; he may have faith, like Claudel, and feel that his earthly duty is to uphold it, or he may, like Eliot, have a sense of tradition together with the belief that he belongs to a religious and political order, which, though shaken, still lives, and free from any propaganda consciousness, he may be first and foremost a poet. There are many other tendencies in poetry and in life to-day, but one could run the risk of asserting that two main trends prevail. Both are historical developments of trends already present in the preceding period. They are Catholicism, coupled with neo-Classicism, and Marxism. The first is partly a reaction to Romanticism, and consists in the desire for order in politics and for more importance to be given to the intellect in the arts ; the second is a kind of refinement of realism in politics and the arts.

Modern consciousness seems to be craving for some kind

of order, and both those creeds offer order, though through different methods and with different principles. The one seeks perhaps the order of the Middle Ages, the age of the theocentric state with a recognized hierarchy and a higher purpose in life, or of Greek democracy and the grace and purity of Grecian lines, forgetting too easily Abelard and the Inquisition, and the internecine wars which destroyed Greece. The other wants in the name of prosperity to reduce life to a scientific experiment and to measure happiness by the law of the greatest common denominator, while the arts should praise the achievements of science and the harmonies of Communism. There remain between those two groups, the puritan conscience soaked in individualism, the Christian existentialists, and the liberal neo-Thomists, who feel that each individual retains his Pascalian greatness, that discipline is only a means and not an end, and that human happiness requires more than material comfort.

The world is torn between two great poles of attraction, liberty and material comfort. The problem is to reconcile them. Man's spiritual life has been more and more worn away by social life and by mechanization, and now he is asked to transfer his allegiance from God, the gods, or simply humanist principles, to machines and statistics. But the kind of humanism which is now advocated has already been proved false by the outcome of the theories of Nietzsche and Marx. The cult of the Superman has led to ruthlessness, and un-adulterated economics can lead to the same ruthlessness. Hegel made possible Marx and also Kierkegaard, who restored to man his importance; he did not, of course, make of him the centre of the universe, but neither did he make of him a mere grain of sand in the communal social structure. The philosophy of dread is now spreading fast towards despair, and, according to its most vigorous exponents, man stands alone, a point in time and in the cosmos which science analyses and decomposes into its smallest particles. Successive devastating wars have shown the state of decay in which humanism was, and have shattered our civilization.

From the end of the Romantic age to modern times, there has been a progressive increase of self-consciousness in the arts, self-consciousness which at times has been more than tinged with social and political or moral preachings. That self-consciousness, which appears already in Heine and probably began as a reaction to the exuberance of the Romantics, seems to have led poetry into rather narrow by-ways. When one thinks of the kind of faith which animated some of those who, in 1914, thought that they were going to fight the war to end wars, and of the sufferings and disappointments which followed it, one is not surprised that something in the human consciousness has withered away, and that men have lost the confidence and boldness of the Romantic age.

After the end of the first world war the artist became more and more conscious of the lack of stability of the world in which he lived and of its blatant iniquities. He felt that while he was still a member of a privileged class in a background of misery, the world was in turmoil. The Communist revolution, the war in China, the rumblings of the Spanish revolution followed one another, and so, by the middle of the 'thirties, the artist had developed a strong political consciousness with tendencies towards the Left, which coincided on the whole with Surrealism in art.

In general, poetic revolutions do not take place in revolutionary periods, but, on the contrary, in moments of internal peace. In the course of revolutions, poets tend to become orators, propagandists, or men of action, and the song becomes a battle cry or a proclamation, but has not much to do with poetry.

> I mastered myself
> and trod
> on the throat
> of my very own song,

said Mayakovski, who knew what it meant to be a poet amid flag-bearers. Poets must concern themselves with poetry ; that does not mean the ivory tower or art for art's sake, but it means, as Goethe said, that " Art is exact sensuous imagination . . . poetry presupposes in the man who is to make it a certain good-natured simplemindedness, in love with the real as the hiding place of the absolute. The higher demands, imposed from above, only destroy his creative state of innocence and put, for the sake of nothing but poetry, in the place of poetry something which is, once and for all, no poetry whatsoever."

Poetry must therefore rise from the thing itself, and that search for the absolute is a return to the essence of language with its incantative and imaginative power. The problem in our time is that language is fragmented ; it is no longer one, and yet, if it is to be efficient it has to cover the whole field of human experience and rise above a reality which is worn out and debased by thousands of years of familiarity. Words have to regain the freshness of the primal dawn and yet be understood in the mature age of the machine ; they have to be what life is both in time and out of time ; they have to be the ever-changing meeting-point of what is and what is not, the instruments to summon worlds whose reality is not that of the eyes, of the ears, but which belongs to what Blake described as the divine faculty—imagination. " What is now proved was once only imagined . . . the poetic genius is the true man . . . the world of imagination is the world of eternity." In spite of the discovery of atomic energy, the equations of Einstein or the new cosmology, the fundamental problems of the source of being, which on the metaphysical plane is also the problem of the essence of language, remains the same. What is also the same as before, and is likely to remain so, is the sense of tragedy born from the fact that man, finite being, lives beset with the constant awareness of the necessity which surrounds him and will one day overwhelm him and restore him to an infinite, whose dim presence in life gnaws ceaselessly his consciousness. These feelings have been, and remain, the background of poetry, which, however much one may admire science or be socially conscious, must endeavour to rediscover in language the great myths and symbols which form the human consciousness. Although we may be living in a sceptical age, that belief in mystery together with the acceptance of the existence of an aura of transcendence, seem to remain the fundamental conditions of poetry, or of any other form of art which, as a creation of the imagination, is both what is and what is not, and is a link with the ideal world whose vague, indefinable memory tinges with sadness our artistic pleasures revealing to us glimmers of a beauty which does not belong to this world. " Our art ", Dante used to say, " is the grandchild of God." Art goes spontaneously to God, and there are strong analogies between the world of art and the world illumined by Divine Grace which is also the world of sainthood.

In our times, men have been disillusioned ; they no more dare to show their inner feelings ; they are too afraid of being laughed at, for sentiments are easily condemned as sentimentality, and so the best thing to do is to hide them by associating them with a humorous remark or a clown-like pirouette. The fear of being taken seriously and laughed at is latent in most of the poetry between the two world wars. Thence the care that poets took of always tempering seriousness with humour, and of transposing one mood into another. " I have measured out my life with coffee spoons," said Prufrock, and the early poetry of T. S. Eliot is full of examples of that admixture of trivial and beautiful, of enthusiasm and reason, of admiration and disgust, until in his later poetry he reaches the perfect blend of feelings and thoughts characteristic of metaphysical poetry, and with the " Four Quartets " he stands above himself and the universe in a kind of Shakespearian grandeur, and the music of his words succeeds in merging man into the cosmos. W. H. Auden is perhaps the best example of that blend of sentiment and satire, seriousness and mockery, and even a kind of puckishness. In France, the best example is Michaux.

This introspective self-consciousness is probably responsible for a renewal of a certain amount of Byzantinism in the arts and also for Surrealism, the aim of which is the abolition of consciousness and the bringing together side by side of the most unexpected associations and unrelated objects. Surrealism might succeed in doing away with certain inhibitions and thus prepare the way for a freer consciousness. Dylan Thomas, who could be described as the best representative of neo-Romanticism, because of his lack of self-consciousness and because of his subjectivity, has travelled along that road. One striking point which emerges from a survey of the modern consciousness is the complete lack of predominant traits and the confusion of the *genre* which transcends all forms of neo-Classicism and neo-Romanticism. The mixture of overintellectualism and romanticism which characterizes our age may be for the moment one of the reasons for the scarcity of great works.

Great poetry seems to have flourished only when strong philosophical or metaphysical convictions were the binding elements which gave reality to life. The first half of the nineteenth century was certainly an age of great ideals and strong convictions and, in spite of a great fragmentation of life and thought, an age which produced great poetry. The discoveries of science gave the second half of the nineteenth century a brief spell of faith in the improvement of the human lot and in the progress of mankind. But it did not last for long, and the twentieth century has proved to be, up till now, an age of bewilderment and disillusion, an age of scientific and spiritual disintegration, an age in which there seem to be no absolutes, an age in which neither Leopardi nor Leibnitz could have lived, for there is neither desperate pessimism nor guiding hope.

The poetry of this age reflects its transiency, its incertitudes, and the atmosphere of unreality which prevails over everything. Science has ground most poetic symbols to lifeless particles, and the poet finds himself faced with a new world, which the poetic imagination has not yet been able, through images and symbols, to mould into its quintessential representation. Science has destroyed part of the old religious faith, and no faith in science or in its materialism, however strong it may be, can be fused into great poetic creations. The poet has the feeling of living amongst inhuman forces which can only crush his sensitiveness if he does not protect it. The introspective hesitations of " La Jeune Parque " are the hesitations of the age, and the poet does not dare to be himself, unafraid of the sun, unmindful of laughter, and capable of speaking for his age and to his age with the depth of feeling and sincerity which T. S. Eliot has succeeded in showing in his later poetry from " Ash Wednesday " to the " Four Quartets ".

Ezra Pound's theories of imagism continue to find some adherents amongst modern poets. Bergson's theories of the moving consciousness and the importance of intuition, together with the extreme subjectivity of the existentialist philosophy which has acquired a great influence nowadays, point the way towards a revival of Romanticism. The gap between faith and materialism is becoming wider and wider, and threatens to lead to open conflict between the political parties who uphold them. The sense of wonder, the importance of the " numinous ", has been lost, and modern consciousness, obsessed by the secrets of life which no psychoanalysis has unfolded yet, is tormented and tossed about between hope and despair, between the need for something to cling to and the desire of new flights and new visions. Carlyle, Wagner, Nietzsche, and Shaw have shown that reason alone cannot save man, and also how man's will has shaped history and influenced his destiny. On the other hand, the last two world catastrophes have shown once more the danger of the excesses of the will uncontrolled by reason, embodied in popular representations. Therefore man's journey towards the future will have to take place along new roads, towards lands where the artist, liberated from his self-consciousness and introversion, will reach towards the vision of eternal Man.

SELECTED LIST OF WORKS

PAUL VALERY

Editions de la N.R.F., copyright by Librairie Gallimard, Paris.

POETRY

Poésies.

DRAMA

Mon Faust.

PROSE WORKS

Eupalinos ou l'Architecte.
L'âme et la danse.
Dialogue de l'Arbre.
Monsieur Teste.
L'ange.
L'idée fixe.
Degas, danse, dessin.
Mauvaises pensées et autres.
Mélange.
Introduction à la Poétique.
Pièces sur l'art.
Regards sur le monde actuel et autres essais.
Variété I to V.
Tel Quel I and II.

JULES SUPERVIELLE

Editions de la N.R.F., copyright by Librairie Gallimard, Paris.

POETRY

Gravitations.
Saisir.
Le Forçat innocent.

Les Amis Inconnus.
La Fable du Monde.
1939–1945.
Choix de poèmes.
Oublieuse Mémoire.
Naissances.

DRAMA

La Belle au Bois.
Comme il vous plaira.
Bolivar.
La Première Famille.
Robinson.
Shéhérazade.
Le Voleur d'Enfants.

NOVELS AND SHORT STORIES

L'Homme de la Pampa.
Le Voleur d'Enfants.
Le Survivant.
L'Enfant de la Haute Mer.
L'Arche de Noé.

PAUL CLAUDEL

Editions de la N.R.F., copyright by Librairie Gallimard, Paris.

POETRY

Cinq grandes odes.
Poèmes et Paroles.
Cantate à trois voix.
Feuilles de Saints.

DRAMA

L'Endormie.
Tête d'Or.
La Ville.
La Jeune Fille Violaine.
L'Échange.
Le Repos du Septième jour.
Partage de Midi.

L'Annonce faite à Marie.
L'Otage.
Protée.
Le Pain Dur.
Le Père Humilié.
La Nuit de Noël 1914.
L'Ours et la Lune.
L'Homme et son Désir.
La Femme et son Ombre.
Le Soulier de Satin.
La Parabole du Festin.
Sous le Rempart d'Athènes.
Le Livre de Christophe Colomb.
Jeanne d'Arc au Bûcher.
L'Histoire de Tobie et de Sara.
La Lune à la recherche d'Elle-même.

TRANSLATIONS OF ÆSCHYLUS

Agamemnon.
Les Choéphores.
Les Euménides.

CRITICISM

Figures et Paraboles.
Art Poétique.
Connaissance de l'Est.
Positions et Propositions, I et II.

PIERRE EMMANUEL

POETRY

Tombeau d'Orphée.	*Egloff, L.U.F.*
Combats avec tes Défenseurs.	,,
La Colombe.	,,
Sodome.	,,
Chansons du Dé à Coudre.	,,
Elégies.	*Cahiers des Poètes, Brussels.*
Le Poète et son Christ.	*Les Cahiers du Rhône.*
XX Cantos.	*Editions Fontaine.*
Tristesse, ô ma Patrie.	,,
Jour de Colère.	*Editions Charlot.*
Orphiques.	*Librairie Gallimard.*
Cantos.	*Ides et Calends.*
La Liberté guide nos pas.	*Poésie '46, Editions Pierre Seghers.*

PROSE

Qui est cet Homme.	*Egloff, L.U.F.*
Poésie Raison Ardente.	"

PAUL ELUARD

Choix de Poèmes.	*Editions de la N.R.F., copyright*
Les Animaux et leurs Hommes, les	*by Librairie Gallimard, Paris.*
Hommes et leurs Animaux.	"
Répétitions.	"
Mourir de ne pas Mourir.	"
" Au Défaut du Silence.	"
Capitale de la Douleur.	"
Défense de Savoir.	"
L'Amour la Poésie.	"
Comme Deux Gouttes d'Eau.	"
La Rose Publique.	"
Chanson complète.	"
Donner à voir.	"
Choix de Poèmes, 1914–41.	"
Poésie ininterrompue.	"
Poèmes politiques.	"
Nuits Partagées.	*Editions G.L.M.*
Facile.	"
La Barre d'Appui.	"
Les Yeux Fertiles.	"
L'Evidence Poétique.	"
Quelques-uns des mots qui jusqu'ici	"
m'étaient mystérieusement interdits.	
Le livre ouvert I, 1938–40.	*Editions des Cahiers d'Art.*
Le livre ouvert II, 1939–41.	"
Le temps déborde.	"
A Toute épreuve.	*Editions des Cahiers libres.*
Dors.	"
La Vie Immédiate.	"
Les Dessous d'une Vie ou La Pyra-	*Les Cahiers du Sud.*
mide Humaine.	
Le lit la table.	*Editions des Trois Collines, Geneva.*
A Pablo Picasso.	"
Voir.	"
Lingères légères.	*Editions Pierre Seghers.*
Corps mémorable.	"
Dignes de Vivre.	*Editions Séquene*
Cours naturel.	*Editions du Sagittaire.*

Le meilleur choix de poèmes est celui que l'on fait pour soi (1818–1918).	*Editions du Sagittaire.* *(Anthology)*
Poésie et vérité 1942.	*La Baconnière, Neuchâtel.*
Au rendez-vous allemand.	*Editions de Minuit.*
Les mains libres.	*Edition Jeanne Bucher.*
Une longue réflexion amoureuse.	*Editions Ides et Calends, Neuchâtel.*
Souvenirs de la maison des fous.	*Editions Vrille.*
Les nécessités de la vie et les conséquences des rêves.	*Editions Lumière, Brussels.*
Le dur désir de durer.	*Editions Arnold-Bordas.*
Objet des mots et des images.	*Editions Opéra.*
Picasso à Antibes.	*Editions René Drouin.*
Perspectives.	*Editions Maeght.*

ST. JOHN PERSE

Editions de la N.R.F., copyright by Librairie Gallimard, Paris.

Pluies.
Exil.
Anabase.

HENRI MICHAUX

Premiers textes.	*Editions du Disque Vert.*
Fables des origines.	,,
Qui je fus. *Collection " Une œuvre, un portrait ".*	*Editions de la N.R.F., copyright by Librairie Gallimard, Paris.*
Ecuador.	,,
La nuit remue.	,,
Un barbare en Asie.	,,
Voyage en Grande Garabagne. *Collection " Métamorphoses ".*	,,
"Plume" and Lointain intérieur.	,,
Au pays de la magie.	,,
Arbres des tropiques.	,,
L'espace du dedans.	,,
Epreuves, exorcismes.	,,
Ailleurs.	,,
La vie dans les plis.	,,
Exorcismes.	*Editions R. Godet.*
Labyrinthes.	,,
Sifflets dans le temple. *Collection " Repères ".*	*Editions G.L.M.*
Peintures.	,,

Apparitions. *Collection " Le Calligraphe ".*	*Editions du " Point du Jour ".*
Peintures et dessins.	„
Meidosems.	„
Mes Propriétés.	*Editions Fourcade.*
Un certain Plume.	*Editions du Carrefour.*
Le lobe des monstres.	*Editions de l'Arbalète.*
Liberté d'action. *Collection L'Age d'Or.*	*Editions Fontaine.*
Ici, Poddema.	*Mermod, Lausanne.*
Arriver à se reveiller.	*Saint-Maurice d'Etelan.*
Nous deux encore.	*J. Lambert et Cie.*
Poésie pour pouvoir.	*H. Drouin.*
Entre centre et absence.	*H. Matarasso.*
Les rêves et la jambe.	*Ça ira, Anvers.*
Tu vas être père, *sous le nom de* " Plume ".